HOW TO

SHOOT YOUR M16/AR-15 IN TRAINING AND COMBAT

PALADIN PRESS • BOULDER, COLORADO

How to Shoot Your M16/AR-15 in Training and Combat

Copyright © 1996 by Paladin Press

ISBN 13: 978-0-87364-888-2
Printed in the United States of America

Published by Paladin Press, a division of
Paladin Enterprises, Inc.
Gunbarrel Tech Center
7077 Winchester Circle
Boulder, Colorado 80301 USA
+1.303.443.7250

Direct inquiries and/or orders to the above address.

PALADIN, PALADIN PRESS, and the "horse head" design
are trademarks belonging to Paladin Enterprises and
registered in United States Patent and Trademark Office.

Visit our Web site at www.paladin-press.com

CONTENTS

CHAPTER 1

Introduction

The procedures and methods used in the Army rifle marksmanship program are based on the concept that soldiers must be skilled marksmen who can effectively apply their firing skills in combat. FM 25-100 stresses marksmanship as a paramount soldier skill. The basic firing skills and exercises outlined in this manual must be a part of every unit's marksmanship training program. Unit commanders must gear their advanced marksmanship training programs to their respective METLs. The proficiency attained by a soldier depends on the proper training and application of basic marksmanship fundamentals. During initial marksmanship training, emphasis is on learning the firing fundamentals, which are taught in a progressive program to prepare soldiers for combat-type exercises.

TRAINING STRATEGY

Training strategy is the overall concept for integrating resources into a program to train individual and collective skills needed to perform a unit's wartime mission.

Training strategies for rifle marksmanship are implemented in TRADOC institutions (IET, NCOES, basic and advanced officer's courses) and in units. The overall training strategy is multifaceted and is inclusive of the specific strategies used in institution and unit programs. Also included are the supporting strategies that use resources such as publications, ranges, ammunition, training aids, devices, simulators, and simulations. These strategies focus on developing critical soldier skills, and on leader skills that are required for success in combat.

Two primary components compose the training strategies: **initial training** and **sustainment training**. Both may include individual and collective skills. Initial training is critical. A task that is taught correctly and learned well is retained longer and skills can be quickly regained and sustained. Therefore, initial training must be taught correctly the first time. However, eventually an individual or unit loses skill proficiency. This learning decay depends on many factors such as the difficulty and complexity of the task. Personnel turnover is a main factor in decay of collective skills, since the loss of critical team members requires retraining to regain proficiency. If a long period elapses between initial and sustainment training sessions or training doctrine is altered, retraining may be required.

The training strategy for rifle marksmanship begins in IET and continues in the unit. An example of this overall process is illustrated in Figure 1-1 and provides a concept of the flow of unit sustainment training (Appendix A). IET provides field units with soldiers who have been trained and who have demonstrated proficiency to standard in basic marksmanship tasks. The soldier graduating from these courses has been trained to maintain the rifle and to hit a point target. He has learned target detection, application of marksmanship fundamentals, and other skills needed to engage a target. The specific tasks and programs taught in IET are explained in Appendix A, FM 21-3, and in commanders' manuals.

FM 23-9

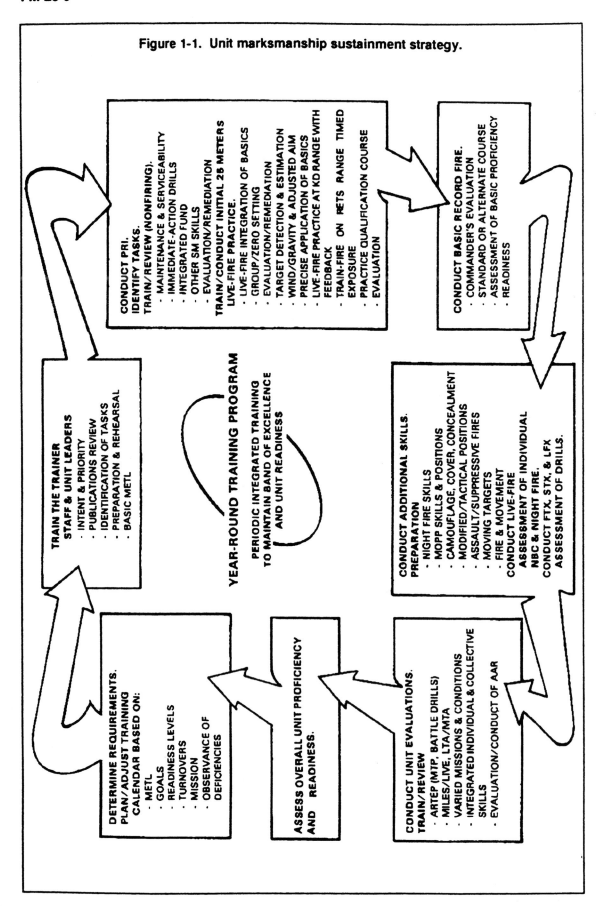

Figure 1-1. Unit marksmanship sustainment strategy.

Training continues in units on the basic skills taught in IET. Additional skills such as area fire are trained and then integrated into collective training exercises, which include platoon and squad live-fire STXs. (A year-round unit marksmanship training program is explained in Appendix A.) The strategy for sustaining the basic marksmanship skills taught in IET is periodic preliminary rifle instruction, followed by instructional and qualification range firing. However, a unit must set up a year-round program to sustain skills. Key elements include training of trainers, refresher training of nonfiring skills, and use of the Weaponeer or other devices for remedial training.

Additional skills trained in the unit include semiautomatic and automatic area fires, night fire, MOPP firing, and moving target training techniques. Related soldier skills of camouflage, cover and concealment, fire and movement, and preparation and selection of a fighting position are addressed in FM 21-3, which must be integrated into tactical training.

In the unit, individual and leader proficiency of marksmanship tasks are integrated into collective training to include squad, section, and platoon drills and STXs; and for the collective tasks in these exercises, and how they are planned and conducted, are in the MTP and battle drills books for each organization. (Force-on-force exercises using MILES are discussed in detail in TC 25-6). Based on the type organization, collective tasks are evaluated to standard and discussed during leader and trainer after-action reviews. Objective evaluations of both individual and unit proficiency provide readiness indicators and future training requirements.

A critical step in the Army's overall marksmanship training strategy is to train the trainers and leaders first. Leader courses and unit publications develop officer and NCO proficiencies necessary to plan and conduct marksmanship training and to evaluate the effectiveness of unit marksmanship programs. Training support materials are provided by the proponent schools to include field manuals, training aids, devices, simulators, and programs that are doctrinal foundations and guidance for training the force.

Once the soldier understands the weapon and has demonstrated skill in zeroing, additional live-fire training and a target acquisition exercise at various ranges are conducted. Target types and scenarios of increasing difficulty must be mastered to develop proficiency.

Initial individual training culminates in the soldier's proficiency assessment, which is conducted on the standard record fire range or approved alternates. This evaluation also provides an overview of unit proficiency and training effectiveness.

General marksmanship training knowledge and firing well are acquired skills, which perish easily. Skill practice should be conducted for short periods throughout the year. Most units have a readiness requirement that all soldiers must zero their rifles within a certain time after unit assignment. Also, soldiers must confirm the zeros of their assigned rifles before conducting a qualification firing. Units should conduct preliminary training and practice firing throughout the year due to personnel turnover. A year-round marksmanship sustainment program is needed for the unit to maintain the individual and collective firing proficiency requirements to accomplish its mission (see Appendix A).

COMBAT FACTORS

The ultimate goal of a unit rifle marksmanship program is well-trained marksmen. In order for a unit to survive and win on the battlefield, the trainer must realize that rifle qualification is not an end but a step toward reaching this combat requirement. To reach this goal, the soldier should consider some of the factors of combat conditions.

- Enemy personnel are seldom visible except when assaulting.

- Most combat fire must be directed at an area where the enemy has been detected or where he is suspected of being located but cannot be seen. Area targets consist of objects or outlines of men irregularly spaced along covered and concealed areas (ground folds, hedges, borders of woods).

- Most combat targets can be detected by smoke, flash, dust, noise, or movement and are visible only for a moment.

- Some combat targets can be engaged by using nearby objects as reference points.

- The range at which enemy soldiers can be detected and effectively engaged rarely exceeds 300 meters.

- The nature of the target and irregularities of terrain and vegetation may require a firer to use a variety of positions in addition to the prone or supported position to fire effectively on the target. In a defensive situation, the firer usually fires from a supported position.

- Choosing an aiming point in elevation is difficult due to the low contrast outline and obscurity of most combat targets.

- Time-stressed fire in combat can be divided into three types:

  - A single, fleeing target that must be engaged quickly.

  - Area targets that must be engaged with distributed fires that cover the entire area. The firer must maintain sustained fire on the sector he is assigned.

  - A surprise target that must be engaged at once with accurate, instinctive fire.

CHAPTER 2

Operation and Function

The procedures and techniques described in this chapter provide commanders, planners, and trainers information on the M16A1 and M16A2 rifles. These include mechanical training, operation, functioning, preventive maintenance, and common malfunctions. Technical data are presented in a logical sequence from basic to the more complex. Additional information is provided in technical manuals for the rifle.

CLEAR the RIFLE

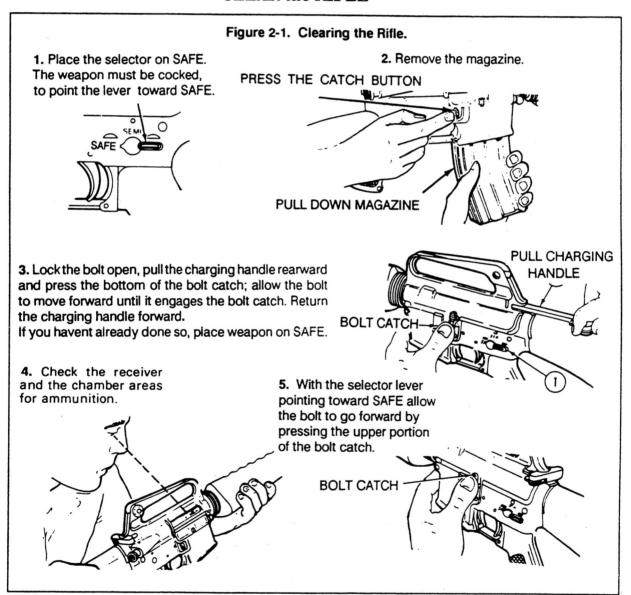

Figure 2-1. Clearing the Rifle.

1. Place the selector on SAFE. The weapon must be cocked, to point the lever toward SAFE.

SAFE

2. Remove the magazine.

PRESS THE CATCH BUTTON

PULL DOWN MAGAZINE

3. Lock the bolt open, pull the charging handle rearward and press the bottom of the bolt catch; allow the bolt to move forward until it engages the bolt catch. Return the charging handle forward.
If you havent already done so, place weapon on SAFE.

PULL CHARGING HANDLE

BOLT CATCH

4. Check the receiver and the chamber areas for ammunition.

5. With the selector lever pointing toward SAFE allow the bolt to go forward by pressing the upper portion of the bolt catch.

BOLT CATCH

Section I. OPERATIONAL CHARACTERISTICS

This section describes general characteristics of the M16A1 and M16A2 rifles.

M16A1 RIFLE
The M16A1 rifle (Figure 2-2) is a 5.56-mm, magazine-fed, gas-operated, shoulder-fired weapon. It is designed for either semiautomatic or automatic fire through the use of a selector lever (SAFE, SEMI, and AUTO).

M16A2 RIFLE
The M16A2 rifle features several product improvements illustrated in this chapter and the operator's manual. The rifle (Figure 2-3) is a 5.56-mm, magazine-fed, gas-operated, shoulder-fired weapon. It is designed to fire either semiautomatic or a three-round burst through the use of a selector lever (SAFE, SEMI, and BURST).

NOTE: The procedures for disassembly, inspection, and maintenance of the M16A1 and M16A2 rifles are contained in the appropriate operator's technical manual.

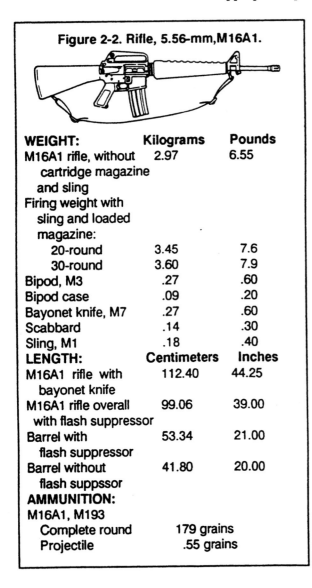

Figure 2-2. Rifle, 5.56-mm, M16A1.

WEIGHT:	Kilograms	Pounds
M16A1 rifle, without cartridge magazine and sling	2.97	6.55
Firing weight with sling and loaded magazine:		
20-round	3.45	7.6
30-round	3.60	7.9
Bipod, M3	.27	.60
Bipod case	.09	.20
Bayonet knife, M7	.27	.60
Scabbard	.14	.30
Sling, M1	.18	.40
LENGTH:	Centimeters	Inches
M16A1 rifle with bayonet knife	112.40	44.25
M16A1 rifle overall with flash suppressor	99.06	39.00
Barrel with flash suppressor	53.34	21.00
Barrel without flash suppssor	41.80	20.00
AMMUNITION:		
M16A1, M193		
Complete round	179 grains	
Projectile	.55 grains	

Figure 2-3. Rifle, 5.56-mm, M16A2.

WEIGHT:	Kilograms	Pounds
M16A2 rifle, without cartridge magazine and sling	3.53	7.78
Firing weight with sling and loaded magazine:		
20-round	3.85	8.48
30-round	3.99	8.79
Bipod, M3	.27	.60
Bipod case	.09	.20
Bayonet knife, M9	.68	1.50
Scabbard	.14	.30
Sling, M1	.18	.40
LENGTH:	Centimeters	Inches
M16A2 rifle with bayonet knife,	113.99	44.88
M16A2 rifle overall with compensator	100.66	39.63
Barrel with compensator	53.34	21.00
Barrel without compensator	41.80	20.00
AMMUNITION:		
M16A2, M855		
Complet e round	190 grains	
Projectile	.62 grains	

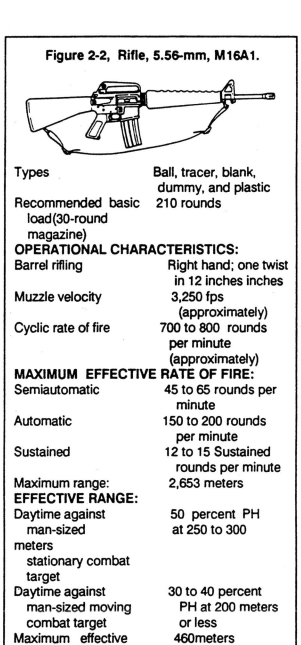

Figure 2-2, Rifle, 5.56-mm, M16A1.

Types	Ball, tracer, blank, dummy, and plastic
Recommended basic load(30-round magazine)	210 rounds

OPERATIONAL CHARACTERISTICS:

Barrel rifling	Right hand; one twist in 12 inches inches
Muzzle velocity	3,250 fps (approximately)
Cyclic rate of fire	700 to 800 rounds per minute (approximately)

MAXIMUM EFFECTIVE RATE OF FIRE:

Semiautomatic	45 to 65 rounds per minute
Automatic	150 to 200 rounds per minute
Sustained	12 to 15 Sustained rounds per minute
Maximum range:	2,653 meters

EFFECTIVE RANGE:

Daytime against man-sized meters stationary combat target	50 percent PH at 250 to 300
Daytime against man-sized moving combat target	30 to 40 percent PH at 200 meters or less
Maximum effective range:	460 meters

Figure 2-3. Rifle, 5.56-mm, M16A2.

Types	Ball, tracer, blank, dummy, and plastic
Recommended basic load(30-round magazine)	210 rounds

OPERATIONAL CHARACTERISTICS:

Barrel rifling	Right hand; one twist in 7 inches
Muzzle velocity	3,100 fps (approximately)
Cyclic rate of fire	700 to 800 rounds per minute (approximately)

MAXIMUM EFFECTIVE RATE OF FIRE:

Semiautomatic	45 rounds per minute
Automatic (3 round burst)	90 rounds per minute
Sustained	12 to 15 rounds per minute
Maximum range:	3,600 meters

EFFECTIVE RANGE:

Daytime against man-sized stationary combat target	50 percent PH at 250 to300 meters
Daytime against man-sized moving combat target	30 to 40 percent PH at 200 meters combat or less

Maximum effective range:

Point target	550 meters
Area target	800 meters

Section II. FUNCTION

The soldier must understand the rifles' components and the mechanical sequence of events during the firing cycle. The M16A1 rifle is designed to function in either the semiautomatic or automatic mode. The M16A2 is designed to function in either the semiautomatic or three-round burst mode.

STEPS OF FUNCTIONING

The eight steps of functioning (feeding, chambering, locking, firing, unlocking, extracting, ejecting, and cocking) begin after the loaded magazine has been inserted into the weapon.

STEP 1: Feeding (Figure 2-4). As the bolt carrier group moves rearward, it engages the buffer assembly and compresses the action spring into the lower receiver extension. When the bolt carrier group clears the top of the magazine, the expansion of the magazine spring forces the follower and a new round up into the path of the forward movement of the bolt. The expansion of the action spring sends the buffer assembly and bolt carrier group forward with enough force to strip a new round from the magazine.

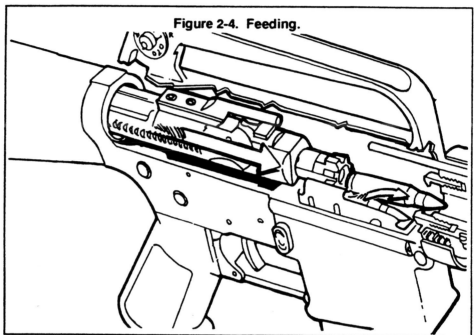

Figure 2-4. Feeding.

STEP 2: Chambering (Figure 2-5). As the bolt carrier group continues to move forward, the face of the bolt thrusts the new round into the chamber. At the same time, the extractor claw grips the rim of the cartridge, and the ejector is compressed.

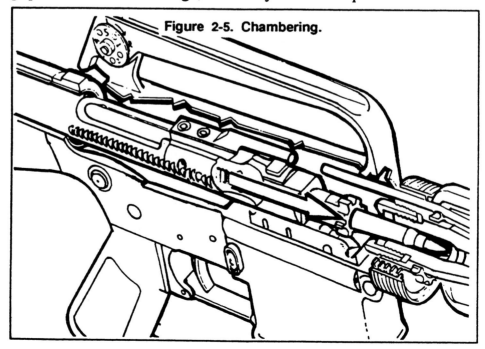

Figure 2-5. Chambering.

STEP 3: Locking (Figure 2-6). As the bolt carrier group moves forward, the bolt is kept in its most forward position by the bolt cam pin riding in the guide channel in the upper receiver. Just before the bolt locking lugs make contact with the barrel extension, the bolt cam pin emerges from the guide channel. The pressure exerted by the contact of the bolt locking lugs and barrel extension causes the bolt cam pin to move along the cam track (located in the bolt carrier) in a counterclockwise direction, rotating the bolt locking lugs in line behind the barrel extension locking lugs. The rifle is then ready to fire.

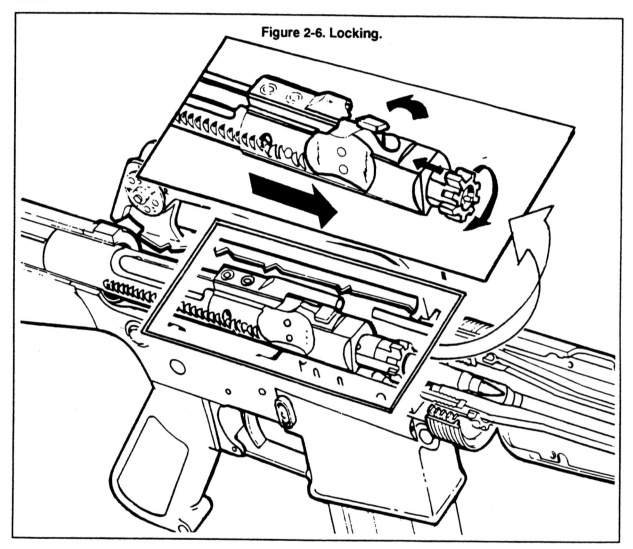

Figure 2-6. Locking.

STEP 4: Firing (Figure 2-7). With a round in the chamber, the hammer cocked, and the selector on SEMI, the firer squeezes the trigger. The trigger rotates on the trigger pin, depressing the nose of the trigger and disengaging the notch on the bottom on the hammer. The hammer spring drives the hammer forward. The hammer strikes the head of the firing pin, driving the firing pin through the bolt into the primer of the round.

When the primer is struck by the firing pin, it ignites and causes the powder in the cartridge to ignite. The gas generated by the rapid burning of the powder forces the projectile from the cartridge and propels it through the barrel. After the projectile has passed the gas port (located on the upper surface of the barrel under the front sight) and before it leaves the barrel, some gas enters the gas port and moves into the gas tube. The gas tube directs the gas into the bolt carrier key and then into the cylinder between the bolt and bolt carrier, causing the carrier to move rearward.

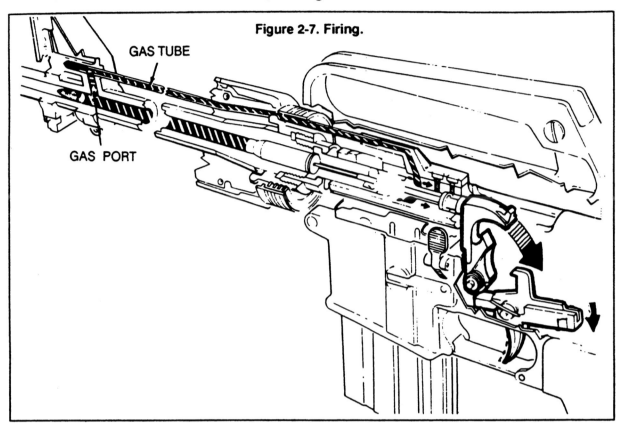

Figure 2-7. Firing.

STEP 5: Unlocking (Figure 2-8). As the bolt carrier moves to the rear, the bolt cam pin follows the path of the cam track (located in the bolt carrier). This action causes the cam pin and bolt assembly to rotate at the same time until the locking lugs of the bolt are no longer in line behind the locking lugs of the barrel extension.

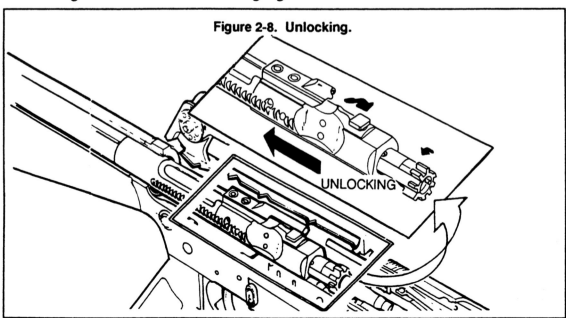

Figure 2-8. Unlocking.

STEP 6: Extracting (Figure 2-9). The bolt carrier group continues to move to the rear. The extractor (which is attached to the bolt) grips the rim of the cartridge case, holds it firmly against the face of the bolt, and withdraws the cartridge case from the chamber.

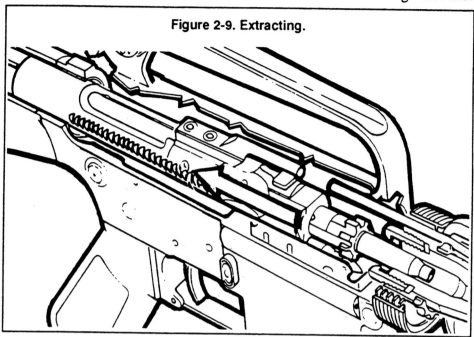

Figure 2-9. Extracting.

STEP 7: Ejecting (Figure 2-10). With the base of a cartridge case firmly against the face of the bolt, the ejector and ejector spring are compressed into the bolt body. As the rearward movement of the bolt carrier group allows the nose of the cartridge case to clear the front of the ejection port, the cartridge is pushed out by the action of the ejector and spring.

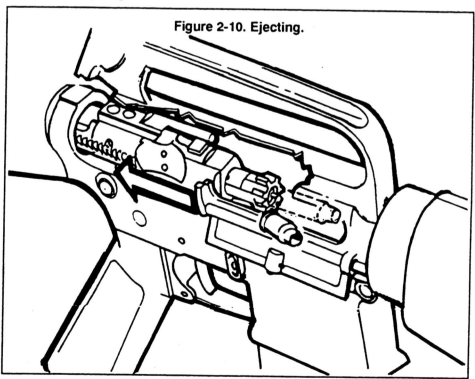

Figure 2-10. Ejecting.

STEP 8: Cocking (Figure 2-11). The rearward movement of the bolt carrier overrides the hammer, forcing it down into the receiver and compressing the hammer spring, cocking the hammer in the firing position. The action of the rifle is much faster than human reaction; therefore, the firer cannot release the trigger fast enough to prevent multiple firing.

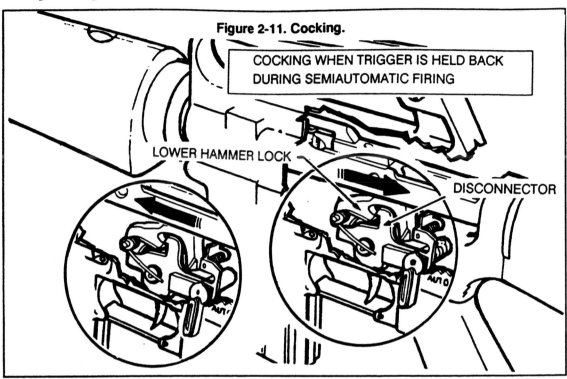

Figure 2-11. Cocking.

COCKING WHEN TRIGGER IS HELD BACK
DURING SEMIAUTOMATIC FIRING

LOWER HAMMER LOCK

DISCONNECTOR

SEMIAUTOMATIC MODE (M16A1 AND M16A2)

The disconnector is mechanism installed so that the firer can fire single rounds in the M16A1 and M16A2 rifles. It is attached to the trigger and is rotated forward by action of the disconnector spring. When the hammer is cocked by the recoil of the bolt carrier, the disconnector engages the lower hook of the hammer and holds it until the trigger is released. Then the disconnector rotates to the rear and down, disengaging the hammer and allowing it to rotate forward until caught by the nose of the trigger. This prevents the hammer from following the bolt carrier forward and causing multiple firing. The trigger must be squeezed again before the next round will fire.

AUTOMATIC FIRE MODE (M16A1)

When the selector lever (Figure 2-12) is set on the AUTO position, the rifle continues to fire as long as the trigger is held back and ammunition is in the magazine. The functioning of certain parts of the rifle changes when firing automatically.

Once the trigger is squeezed and the round is fired, the bolt carrier group moves to the rear and the hammer is cocked. The center cam of the selector depresses the rear of the disconnector and prevents the nose of the disconnector from engaging the lower hammer hook. The bottom part of the automatic sear catches the upper hammer hook and holds it until the bolt carrier group moves forward. The bottom part strikes the top of the sear and releases the hammer, causing the rifle to fire automatically.

If the trigger is released, the hammer moves forward and is caught by the nose of the trigger. This ends the automatic cycle of fire until the trigger is squeezed again.

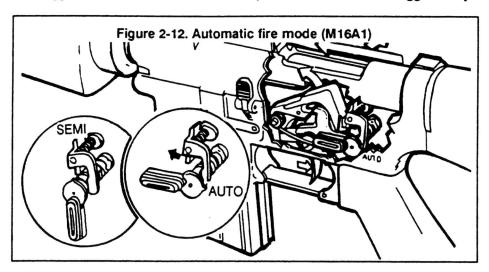

Figure 2-12. Automatic fire mode (M16A1)

BURST FIRE MODE (M16A2)

When the selector lever is set on the BURST position (Figure 2-13), the rifle fires a three-round burst if the trigger is held to the rear during the complete cycle. The weapon continues to fire three-round bursts with each separate trigger pull as long as ammunition is in the magazine. Releasing the trigger or exhausting ammunition at any point in the three-round cycle interrupts fire, producing one or two shots. Reapplying the trigger only completes the interrupted cycle — it does not begin a new one. This is not a malfunction. The M16A2 disconnector has a three-cam mechanism that continuously rotates with each firing cycle. Based on the position of the disconnector cam, the first trigger pull (after initial selection of the BURST position) can produce one, two, or three firing cycles before the trigger must be pulled again. The burst cam rotates until it reaches the stop notch.

NOTE: See the operator's manual for a detailed discussion on the burst position.

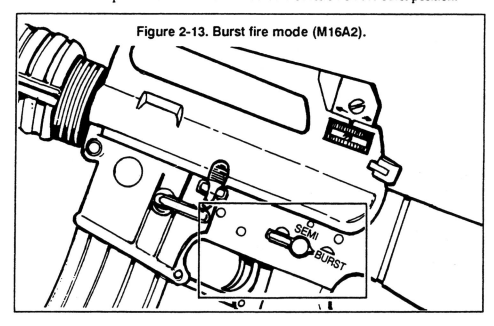

Figure 2-13. Burst fire mode (M16A2).

Section III. MALFUNCTIONS AND CORRECTIONS

Commanders and unit armorers are responsible for the organizational and direct support maintenance of weapons. Soldiers are responsible for keeping their weapons clean and operational at all times — in training and in combat. Therefore, the soldier should be issued an operator's technical manual and cleaning equipment for his assigned weapon.

STOPPAGE

A stoppage is a failure of an automatic or semiautomatic firearm to complete the cycle of operation. The firer can apply immediate or remedial action to clear the stoppage. Some stoppages that cannot be cleared by immediate or remedial action could require weapon repair to correct the problem. A complete understanding of how the weapon functions is an integral part of applying immediate-action procedures.

Immediate Action. This involves quickly applying a possible correction to reduce a stoppage based on initial observation or indicators but without determining the actual cause. To apply immediate action, the soldier would perform these steps: Gently slap upward on the magazine to ensure it is fully seated, and the magazine follower is not jammed. Pull the charging handle fully to the rear and check the chamber (observe for the ejection of a live or expended cartridge). Release the charging handle (do not ride it forward). Strike the forward assist assembly to ensure bolt closure. Try to fire the rifle.

Apply immediate action only one time for a given stoppage. Do not apply immediate action a second time. If the rifle still fails to fire, inspect it to determine the cause of the stoppage or malfunction and take appropriate remedial action.

Remedial Action. Remedial action is the continuing effort to determine the cause for a stoppage or malfunction and to try to clear the stoppage once it has been identified.

> ## WARNING
>
> IF AN AUDIBLE "POP" OR REDUCED RECOIL OCCURS DURING FIRING, IMMEDIATELY CEASE FIRE. THIS POP OR REDUCED RECOIL CAN BE THE RESULT OF A ROUND BEING FIRED WITHOUT ENOUGH FORCE TO SEND THE PROJECTILE OUT OF THE BARREL. DO NOT APPLY IMMEDIATE ACTION. REMOVE THE MAGAZINE, LOCK THE BOLT TO THE REAR, AND PLACE THE SELECTOR LEVER IN THE SAFE POSITION. VISUALLY INSPECT THE BORE TO ENSURE A PROJECTILE IS NOT LODGED IN THE BARREL. IF A PROJECTILE IS LODGED IN THE BARREL, DO NOT TRY TO REMOVE IT. TURN THE RIFLE IN TO THE ARMORER.

MAJOR CATEGORIES OF MALFUNCTIONS

A malfunction is caused by a procedural or mechanical failure of the rifle, magazine, or ammunition. Prefiring checks and serviceability inspections identify potential problems before they become malfunctions. Three primary categories of malfunctions are:

1. Failure to Feed, Chamber, or Lock.

Description. A malfunction can occur when loading the rifle or during the cycle of operation. Once the magazine has been loaded into the rifle, the forward movement of the bolt carrier group could lack enough force (generated by the expansion of the action spring) to feed, chamber, and lock the first round. While firing, the cycle of function is interrupted by a failure to strip a round from the magazine, to chamber the round, and to lock it (Figure 2-14).

Probable causes. The cause could be the result of one or more of the following: excess accumulation of dirt or fouling in and around the bolt and bolt carrier, defective magazine (dented or bulged), magazine improperly loaded. A defective round (projectile forced back into the cartridge case that could result in a "stubbed round") or the base of the previous field cartridge could be separated, leaving the remainder in

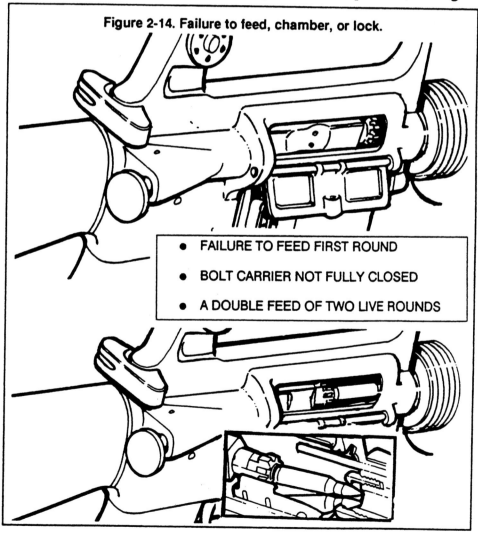

Figure 2-14. Failure to feed, chamber, or lock.

- FAILURE TO FEED FIRST ROUND

- BOLT CARRIER NOT FULLY CLOSED

- A DOUBLE FEED OF TWO LIVE ROUNDS

the chamber. Other causes could be: damaged or broken action spring, exterior accumulation of dirt in the lower receiver extension, or fouled gas tube resulting in short recoil.

Corrective action. Applying immediate action usually corrects the malfunction. However, to avoid the risk of further jamming, the firer should watch for ejection of a cartridge and ensure that the upper receiver is free of any loose rounds. If immediate action fails to clear the malfunction, remedial action must be taken. The carrier should not be forced. If resistance is encountered, which can occur with an unserviceable round, the bolt should be locked to the rear, magazine removed, and malfunction cleared—for example, a bolt override is when a cartridge has wedged itself between the bolt and charging handle. The best way to relieve this problem is by—

- Ensuring that the charging handle is pushed forward and locked in place.

- Holding the rifle securely and pulling the bolt to the rear until the bolt seats completely into the buffer well.

- Turning the rifle upright and allowing the overridden cartridge to fall out.

2. Failure to Fire Cartridge.

Description. Failure of a cartridge to fire despite the fact that a round has been chambered, the trigger is pulled, and the sear has released the hammer. This occurs when the firing pin fails to strike the primer with enough force or when the ammunition is bad.

Probable causes. Excessive carbon buildup on the firing pin (Figure 2-15A) is often the cause, because the full forward travel of the firing pin is restricted. However, a defective or worn firing pin can give the same results. Inspection of the ammunition could reveal a shallow indentation or no mark on the primer, indicating a firing pin problem (Figure 2-15B). Cartridges that show a normal indentation on the primer but did not fire indicate bad ammunition.

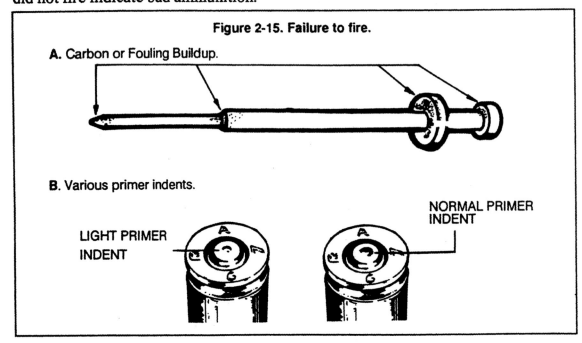

Figure 2-15. Failure to fire.

A. Carbon or Fouling Buildup.

B. Various primer indents.

LIGHT PRIMER INDENT

NORMAL PRIMER INDENT

Corrective action. If the malfunction continues, the firing pin, bolt, carrier, and locking lug recesses of the barrel extension should be inspected, and any accumulation of excessive carbon or fouling should be removed. The firing pin should also be inspected for damage. Cartridges that show a normal indentation on the primer but failed to fire could indicate a bad ammunition lot. Those that show a complete penetration of the primer by the firing pin could also indicate a bad ammunition lot or a failure of the cartridge to fully seat in the chamber.

NOTE: If the round is suspected to be faulty, it is reported and returned to the agency responsible for issuing ammunition

3. Failure to Extract and Eject.

Failure to extract. The cartridge must extract before it can eject.

Description. A failure to extract results when the cartridge case remains in the rifle chamber. While the bolt and bolt carrier could move rearward only a short distance, more commonly the bolt and bolt carrier recoil fully to the rear, leaving the cartridge case in the chamber. A live round is then forced into the base of the cartridge case as the bolt returns in the next feed cycle. This malfunction is one of the hardest to clear.

NOTE: Short recoil can also be caused by a fouled or obstructed gas tube.

WARNING

A FAILURE TO EXTRACT IS CONSIDERED TO BE AN EXTREMELY SERIOUS MALFUNCTION, REQUIRING THE USE OF TOOLS TO CLEAR. A LIVE ROUND COULD BE LEFT IN THE CHAMBER AND BE ACCIDENTALLY DISCHARGED. IF A SECOND LIVE ROUND IS FED INTO THE PRIMER OF THE CHAMBERED LIVE ROUND, THE RIFLE COULD EXPLODE AND CAUSE PERSONAL INJURY. THIS MALFUNCTION MUST BE PROPERLY IDENTIFIED AND REPORTED. FAILURES TO EJECT SHOULD NOT BE REPORTED AS EXTRACTION FAILURES.

Probable cause. Short recoil cycles and fouled or corroded rifle chambers are the most common causes of failures to extract. A damaged extractor or weak/broken extractor spring can also cause this malfunction.

Corrective action. The severity of a failure to extract determines the corrective action procedures. If the bolt has moved rearward far enough so that it strips a live round from the magazine in its forward motion, the bolt and carrier must be locked to the rear.

The magazine and all loose rounds must be removed before clearing the stoppage. Usually, tapping the butt of the rifle on a hard surface causes the cartridge to fall out of the chamber. However, if the cartridge case is ruptured, it can be seized. When this occurs, a cleaning rod can be inserted into the bore from the muzzle end. The cartridge case can be forced from the chamber by tapping the cleaning rod against the inside base of the fired cartridge. When cleaning and inspecting the mechanism and chamber reveal no defects but failures to extract persist, the extractor and extractor spring should be replaced. If the chamber surface is damaged, the entire barrel must be replaced.

Failure to Eject. A failure to eject a cartridge is an element in the cycle of functioning of the rifle, regardless of the mode of fire. A malfunction occurs when the cartridge is not ejected through the ejection port and either remains partly in the chamber or becomes jammed in the upper receiver as the bolt closes. When the firer initially clears the rifle, the cartridge could strike an inside surface of the receiver and bounce back into the path of the bolt.

Probable cause. Ejection failures are hard to diagnose but are often related to a weak or damaged extractor spring and/or ejector spring. Failures to eject can also be caused by a buildup of carbon or fouling on the ejector spring or extractor, or from short recoil. Short recoil is usually due to a buildup of fouling in the carrier mechanism or gas tube, which could result in many failures to include a failure to eject. Resistance caused by a carbon-coated or corroded chamber can impede the extraction, and then the ejection of a cartridge.

Corrective action. While retraction of the charging handle usually frees the cartridge and permits removal, the charging handle must not be released until the position of the next live round is determined. If another live round has been sufficiently stripped from the magazine or remains in the chamber, then the magazine and all live rounds could also require removal before the charging handle can be released. If several malfunctions occur and are not corrected by cleaning and lubricating, the ejector spring, extractor spring, and extractor should be replaced.

OTHER MALFUNCTIONS
Some other malfunctions that can occur are as follows.

- Failure of the bolt to remain in a rearward position after the last round in the magazine is fired. Check for a bad magazine or short recoil.

- Failure of the bolt to lock in the rearward position when the bolt catch has been engaged. Check bolt catch; replace as required.

- Firing two or more rounds when the trigger is pulled and the selection lever is in the SEMI position. This indicates a worn sear, cam, or disconnector. Turn in to armorer to repair and replace trigger group parts as required.

- Trigger will not pull or return after release with the selector set in a firing position. This indicates that the trigger pin (Figure 2-16A) has backed out of the receiver or the hammer spring is broken. Turn in to armorer to replace or repair.

- Failure of the magazine to lock into the rifle (Figure 2-16B). Check the magazine and check magazine catch for damage. Turn in to armorer to adjust the catch; replace as required.

- Failure of any part of the bolt carrier group to function (Figure 2-16C). Check for incorrect assembly of components. Correctly clean and assemble the bolt carrier group, or replace damaged parts.

- Failure of the ammunition to feed from the magazine (Figure 2-16D). Check for damaged magazine. A damaged magazine could cause repeated feeding failures and should be turned in to armorer or exchanged.

NOTE: Additional technical information on troubleshooting malfunctions and repairing components is contained in the organizational and DS maintenance publications and manuals.

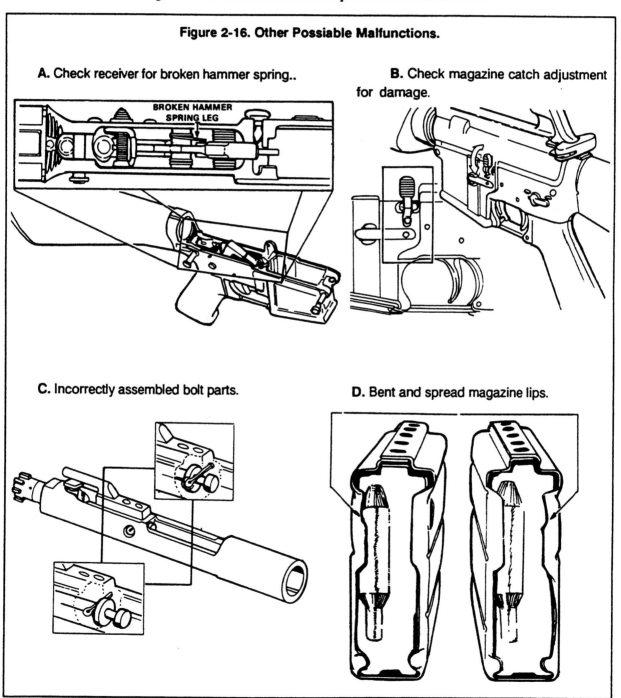

Figure 2-16. Other Possiable Malfunctions.

A. Check receiver for broken hammer spring..

BROKEN HAMMER SPRING LEG

B. Check magazine catch adjustment for damage.

C. Incorrectly assembled bolt parts.

D. Bent and spread magazine lips.

Section IV. AMMUNITION

This section contains information on different types of standard military ammunition used in the M16A1 and M16A2 rifles. Use only authorized ammunition that is manufactured to US and NATO specifications.

TYPES AND CHARACTERISTICS

The characteristics of the M16 family of ammunition are described in this paragraph.

Cartridge, 5.56-mm, Dummy, M199. (Used in both rifles.) The M199 dummy cartridge is used during dry fire and other training (see 3, Figure 2-17). This cartridge can be identified by the six grooves along the side of the case beginning about 1/2 inch from its head. It contains no propellent or primer. The primer well is open to prevent damage to the firing pin.

Cartridge, 5.56-mm, Blank, M200. (Used in the M16A1 or M16A2 rifle.) The M200 blank cartridge has no projectile. The case mouth is closed with a seven-petal rosette crimp and shows a violet tip (see 4, Figure 2-17). (See Appendix C for use of the blank firing attachment.). The original M200 blank cartridge had a white tip. Field use of this cartridge resulted in residue buildup, which caused several malfunctions. Only the violet-tipped M200 cartridge should be used.

Cartridge, 5.56-mm, Plastic Practice Ammunition, M862. (Used in the M16A1 and M16A2 rifles.) The M862 PPA is designed exclusively for training. It can be used in lieu of service ammunition on indoor ranges, and by units that have a limited range fan that does not allow the firing of service ammunition. It is used with the M2 training bolt.

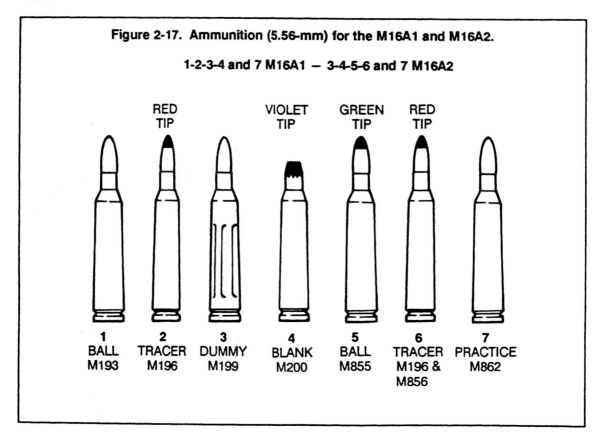

Figure 2-17. Ammunition (5.56-mm) for the M16A1 and M16A2.

1-2-3-4 and 7 M16A1 — 3-4-5-6 and 7 M16A2

Although PPA (see 7, Figure 2-17) closely replicates the trajectory and characteristics of service ammunition out to 25 meters, it should not be used to set the combat battlesight zero of weapons to fire service ammunition. The setting that is placed on the sights for a weapon firing PPA could be different for service ammunition.

If adequate range facilities are not available for sustainment (particularly Reserve Components), PPA can be used for any firing exercises of 25 meters or less. This includes the 25-meter scaled silhouette, 25-meter alternate qualification course, and quick-fire training. Units that have an indoor range with adequate ventilation or MOUT site could use PPA. (See Appendix C for use in training.)

Cartridge, 5.56-mm, Ball, M193. The M193 cartridge is a center-fire cartridge with a 55-grain, gilding-metal, jacketed, lead alloy core bullet. The primer and case are waterproof. The M193 round is the standard cartridge for field use with the M16A1 rifle and has no identifying marks (see 1, Figure 2-17). This cartridge has a projectile weight of 55 grains and is 1.9 cm long, with a solid lead core.

Figure 2-21. Ammunition for 5.56-mm M16A1 (1 through 4 and 7) and M16A2 (3 through 7).

Cartridge, 5.56-mm, Tracer, M196. (Used in the M16A1 rifle.) The M196 cartridge is identified by a red- or orange-painted tip (see 2, Figure 2-17). Its main uses are for observation of fire, incendiary effect, and signaling. Soldiers should avoid long-term use of 100-percent tracer rounds. This could cause deposits of incendiary material/chemical compounds that could cause damage to the barrel. Therefore, when tracer rounds are fired, they are mixed with ball ammunition in a ratio no greater than one-to-one with a preferred ratio of three or four ball rounds to one tracer round.

Cartridge, 5.56-mm, Ball, M855. The M855 cartridge has a 62-grain, gilding-metal, jacketed, lead alloy core bullet with a steel penetrator. The primer and case are waterproof. This is the NATO standard round for the M16A2 rifle (also used in the M249 SAW). It is identified by a green tip (see 5, Figure 2-17). This cartridge has a projectile weight of 62 grains and is 2.3 cm long, with a steel penetrator in the nose.

Cartridge, 5.56-mm, Tracer, M856. (Used in the M16A2 rifle.) The M856 tracer cartridge has similar characteristics as the M196 but slightly longer tracer burnout distance. This cartridge has a 63.7-grain bullet. The M856 does not have a steel penetrator. It is also identified by a red tip (orange when linked 4 and 1) (6, Figure 2-17).

CARE AND HANDLING

When necessary to store ammunition in the open, it must be raised on dunnage at least 6 inches from the ground and protected with a cover, leaving enough space for air circulation. Since ammunition and explosives are adversely affected by moisture and high temperatures, the following must be adhered to:

- Do not open ammunition boxes until ready to use.

- Protect ammunition from high temperatures and the direct rays of the sun.

- Do not attempt to disassemble ammunition or any of its components.

- Never use lubricants or grease on ammunition.

Section V. DESTRUCTION OF MATERIEL

Rifles subject to capture or abandonment in the combat zone are destroyed only by the authority of the unit commander IAW orders of or policy established by the Army commander. The destruction of equipment is reported through regular command channels.

MEANS OF DESTRUCTION

Certain procedures outlined require use of explosives and incendiary grenades. Issue of these and related principles, and specific conditions under which destruction is effected, are command decisions. Of the several means of destruction, the following apply:

- **Mechanical.** Requires axe, pick mattock, sledge, crowbar, or other heavy implement.

- **Burning.** Requires gasoline, oil, incendiary grenades, and other flammables, or welding or cutting torch.

- **Demolition.** Requires suitable explosives or ammunition. Under some circumstances, hand grenades can be used.

- **Disposal.** Requires burying in the ground, dumping in streams or marshes, or scattering so widely as to preclude recovery of essential parts.

It is important that the same parts be destroyed on all like materiel, including spare parts, so that the enemy cannot rebuild one complete unit from several damaged units. If destruction is directed, appropriate safety precautions must be observed.

FIELD-EXPEDIENT METHODS

If destruction of the individual rifle must be performed to prevent enemy use, the rifle must be damaged so it cannot be restored to a usable condition. Expedient destruction requires that key operational parts be separated from the rifle or damaged beyond repair. Priority is given in the following order:

FIRST: **Bolt carrier group**; removed and discarded or hidden.

SECOND: **Upper receiver group**; separated and discarded or hidden.

THIRD: **Lower receiver group**; separated and discarded or hidden.

CHAPTER 3

Rifle Marksmanship Training

The procedures and techniques for implementing the Army rifle marksmanship training program are based on the concept that all soldiers must understand common firing principles, be proficient marksmen, and be confident in applying their firing skills in combat. This depends on their understanding of the rifle and correct application of marksmanship fundamentals. Proficiency is accomplished through practice that is supervised by qualified instructors/trainers and through objective performance assessments by unit leaders. During preliminary training, instructors/trainers emphasize initial learning, reviewing, reinforcing, and practicing of the basics. Soldiers must master weapon maintenance, functions checks, and firing fundamentals before progressing to advanced skills and firing exercises under tactical conditions. The skills the soldier must learn are developed in the following four phases:

- *PHASE I. Preliminary Rifle Instruction.*

- *PHASE II. Downrange Feedback Range Firing.*

- *PHASE III. Field Firing on Train-Fire Ranges.*

- *PHASE IV. Advanced and Collective Firing Exercises.*

Each soldier progresses through these phases to meet the objective of rifle marksmanship training and sustainment. The accomplishment of these phases are basic and necessary in mastering the correct techniques of marksmanship and when functioning as a soldier in a combat area. (See Chapter 1 and Appendix A.)

Section I. BASIC PROGRAM IMPLEMENTATION

Knowledgeable instructors/cadre are the key to marksmanship performance. All commanders must be aware of maintaining expertise in marksmanship instruction/training. (See Appendix D.)

INSTRUCTOR/TRAINER SELECTION

Institutional and unit instructors/trainers are selected and assigned from the most highly qualified soldiers. These soldiers must have an impressive background in rifle marksmanship; be proficient in applying these fundamentals; know the importance of marksmanship training; and have a competent and professional attitude. The commander must ensure that selected instructors/trainers can effectively train other soldiers. Local instructor/trainer training courses and marksmanship certification programs must be established to ensure that instructor/trainer skills are developed.

Cadre/trainer refers to a marksmanship instructor/trainer that has more experience and expertise than the firer. He trains soldiers in the effective use of the rifle by maintaining strict discipline on the firing line, insisting on compliance with range procedures and program objectives, and enforcing safety regulations. A good instructor/trainer must understand the training phases and techniques for developing marksmanship skills, and he must possess the following qualifications:

Knowledge. The main qualifications for an effective instructor/trainer are thorough knowledge of the rifle, proficiency in firing, and understanding supporting marksmanship manuals.

Patience. The instructor/trainer must relate to the soldier calmly, persistently, and patiently.

Understanding. The instructor/trainer can enhance success and understanding by emphasizing close observance of rules and instructions.

Consideration. Most soldiers enjoy firing regardless of their performance and begin with great enthusiasm. The instructor/trainer can enhance this enthusiasm by being considerate of his soldiers feelings and by encouraging firing abilities throughout training, which can also make teaching a rewarding experience.

Respect. An experienced cadre is assigned the duties of instructor/trainer, which classifies him as a technical expert and authority. The good instructor/trainer is alert for mistakes and patiently makes needed corrections.

Encouragement. The instructor/trainer can encourage his soldiers by convincing them to achieve good firing performance through practice. His job is to impart knowledge and to assist the soldier so he can gain the practical experience needed to become a good firer.

DUTIES OF THE INSTRUCTOR/TRAINER

The instructor/trainer helps the firer master the fundamentals of rifle marksmanship. He ensures that the firer consistently applies what he has learned. Then, it is a matter of practice, and the firer soon acquires good firing skills. When training the beginner, the instructor/trainer could confront problems such as fear, nervousness, forgetfulness, failure to understand, and a lack of coordination or determination. An expert firer is often unaware that some problems are complicated by arrogance and carelessness. With all types of firers, the instructor/trainer must ensure that firers are aware of their firing errors, understand the causes, and apply remedies. Sometimes errors are not evident. The instructor/trainer must isolate errors, explain them, and help the firer concentrate on correcting them.

Observing the Firer. The instructor/trainer observes the firer during drills and in the act of firing to pinpoint errors. If there is no indication of probable error, then the firer's position, breath control, shot anticipation, and trigger squeeze are closely observed.

Questioning the Firer. The firer is asked to detect his errors and to explain his firing procedure to include position, aiming, breath control, and trigger squeeze.

Analyzing the Shot Group. This is an important step in detecting and correcting errors. When analyzing a target, the instructor/trainer critiques and correlates observations of the firer to probable errors in performance, according to the shape and size of shot groups. A poor shot group is usually caused by more than one observable error.

NOTE: To assist instructors/trainers, TVTs 7-1 and 7-2 should be viewed before conducting training.

Section II. CONDUCT OF TRAINING

In the conduct of marksmanship training, the instructor/trainer first discusses an overview of the program to include the progression and step-by-step process in developing firing skills. (This can be accomplished by showing TVT 7-13.) Once the soldier realizes the tasks and skills involved, he is ready to begin. He receives preliminary rifle instruction before firing any course. Also during this initial phase, an understanding of the service rifle developes through review.

MECHANICAL TRAINING

Mechanical training includes characteristics and capabilities, disassembly and assembly, operations and functioning, serviceability checks, and weapons maintenance. It also stresses the performance of immediate action to clear or reduce a stoppage, and the safe handling of rifles and ammunition (see Chapter 2). Examples of mechanical training drills, along with tasks, conditions, and standards, are provided in Appendix A. These examples are also used for initial entry training at the Army training centers. Mechanical training must encompass all related tasks contained in the soldier's manual of common tasks (SMCT) to include the correct procedures for disassembly, cleaning, inspection, and reassembly of the rifle and magazine (Figure 3-1).

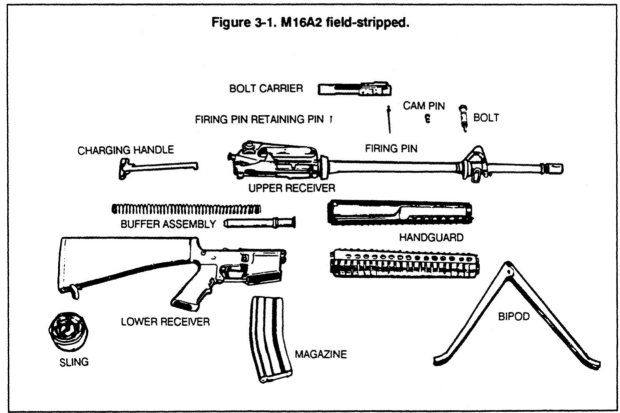

Figure 3-1. M16A2 field-stripped.

Serviceability inspections and preventive maintenance checks must be practiced to ensure soldiers have reliable weapons systems during training and in combat. Technical information necessary to conduct mechanical training is contained in the soldier's operator's manual (M16A1—TM 9-1005-249-10; M16A2—TM 9-1005-319-10). Once the basic procedures have been demonstrated, soldiers should practice the mechanical training skills under varied conditions to include during nighttime, and in MOPP and arctic clothing.

As part of mechanical training, soldiers must be taught and must practice procedures for properly loading ammunition into magazines to include both single loose rounds and speed loading of 10-round clips (Figure 3-2).

Figure 3-2. Loading and unloading magazine.

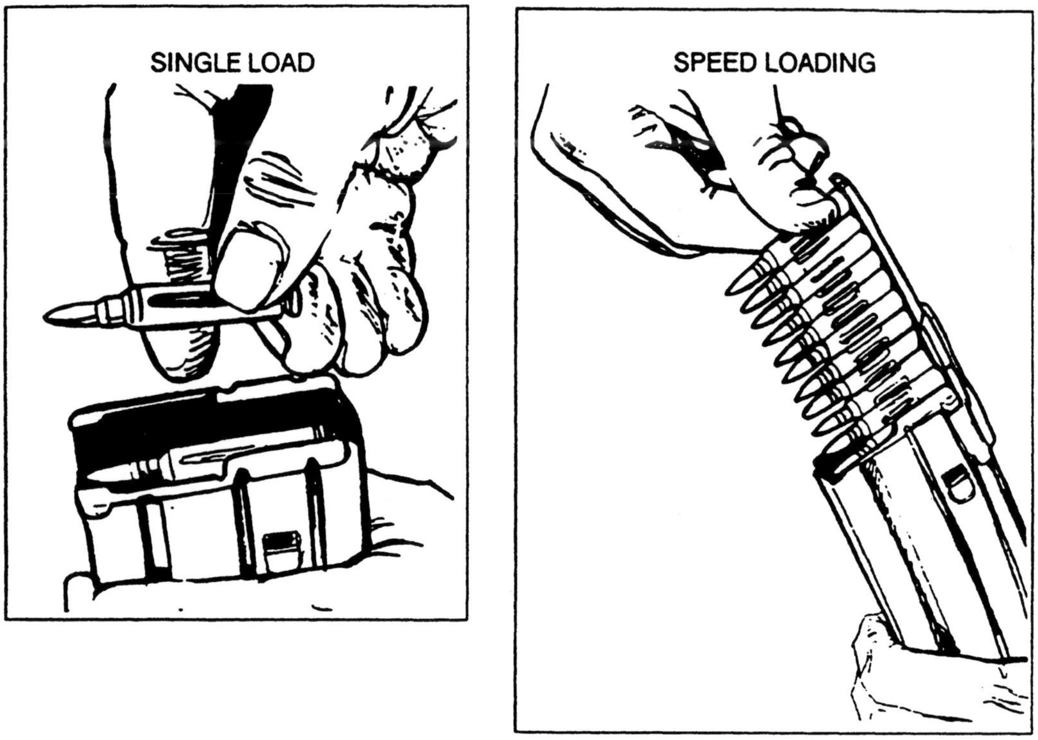

SINGLE LOAD

SPEED LOADING

Emphasis on maintenance and understanding of the rifle can prevent most problems and malfunctions. However, a soldier could encounter a stoppage or malfunction. The soldier must quickly correct the problem by applying immediate action and continue to place effective fire on the target.

Immediate-action procedures contained in Chapter 2 and the operator's technical manual should be taught and practiced as part of preliminary dry-fire exercises, and should be reinforced during live-fire exercises.

Immediate-action drills should be conducted using dummy ammunition (M199) loaded into the magazine. The soldier chamber the first dummy round and assume a firing position. When he squeezes the trigger and the hammer falls with no recoil, this is the cue to apply the correct immediate-action procedure and to refire. Drill should continue until soldiers can perform the task in three to five seconds.

The word **SPORTS** is a technique for assisting the soldier in learning the proper procedures for applying immediate action to the M16A1 and M16A2 rifles.

First, **THINK**, then:

Slap up on the bottom of the magazine.

Pull the charging handle to the rear.

Observe the chamber for an ejection of the round.

Release the charging handle.

Tap the forward assist.

Squeeze the trigger again.

NOTE: When slapping up on the magazine, be careful not to knock a round out of the magazine into the line of the bolt carrier, causing more problems. Slap hard enough only to ensure the magazine is fully seated.

MARKSMANSHIP FUNDAMENTALS

The soldier must understand the four key fundamentals before he approaches the firing line. He must be able to establish a **steady position** that allows observation of the target. He must **aim** the rifle at the target by aligning the sight system, and he must fire the rifle without disturbing this alignment by improper **breathing** or during **trigger squeeze**. The skills needed to accomplish these are known as **rifle marksmanship fundamentals**. These simple procedures aid the firer in achieving target hits under many conditions when expanded with additional techniques and information. Applying these four fundamentals rapidly and consistently is called the **integrated act of firing**.

Steady Position. When the soldier approaches the firing line, he should assume a comfortable, steady firing position in order to hit targets consistently. The time and supervision each soldier has on the firing line are limited (illustrated on the following page in Figure 3-3). Therefore, he must learn how to establish a steady position during dry-fire training. The firer is the best judge as to the quality of his position. If he can hold the front sight post steady through the fall of the hammer, he has a good position. The steady position elements are as follows:

Nonfiring hand grip. The rifle handguard rests on the heel of the hand in the V formed by the thumb and fingers. The grip of the nonfiring hand is light, and slight rearward pressure is exerted.

Rifle butt position. The butt of the stock is placed in the pocket of the firing shoulder. This reduces the effect of recoil and helps ensure a steady position.

Firing hand grip. The firing hand grasps the pistol grip so that it fits the V formed by the thumb and forefinger. The forefinger is placed on the trigger so that the lay of the rifle is not disturbed when the trigger is squeezed. A slight rearward pressure is exerted by the remaining three fingers to ensure that the butt of the stock remains in the pocket of the shoulder, thus minimizing the effect of recoil.

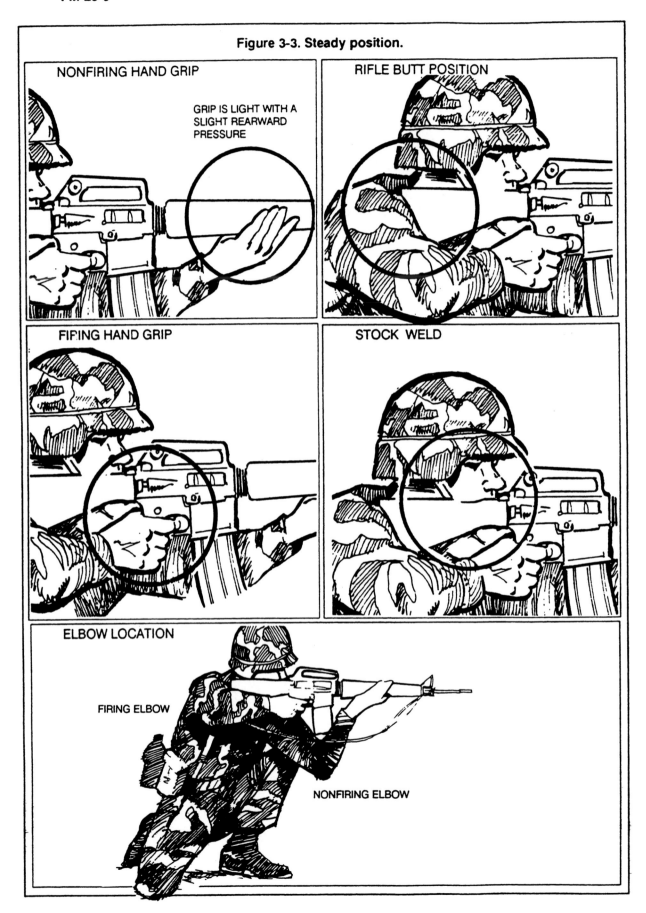

Figure 3-3. Steady position.

Firing elbow placement. The location of the firing elbow is important in providing balance. The exact location, however, depends on the firing/fighting position used — for example, kneeling, prone, or standing. Placement should allow shoulders to remain level.

Nonfiring elbow. The nonfiring elbow is positioned firmly under the rifle to allow for a comfortable and stable position. When the soldier engages a wide sector of fire, moving targets, and targets at various elevations, his nonfiring elbow should remain free from support.

Stock weld. The stock weld is taught as an integral part of various positions. Two key factors emphasized are that the stock weld should provide for a natural line of sight through the center of the rear sight aperture to the front sight post and to the target. The firer's neck should be relaxed, allowing his cheek to fall naturally onto the stock. Through dry-fire training, the soldier is encouraged to practice this position until he assumes the same stock weld each time he assumes a given position. This provides consistency in aiming, which is the purpose of obtaining a correct stock weld. Proper eye relief is obtained when a soldier establishes a good stock weld. There is normally a small change in eye relief each time he assumes a different firing position. Soldiers should begin by trying to touch his nose close to the charging handle when assuming a firing position.

Support. If artificial support (sandbags, logs, stumps) is available, it should be used to steady the position and to support the rifle. If it is not available, then the bones, not the muscles, in the firer's upper body must support the rifle.

Muscle relaxation. If support is properly used, the soldier should be able to relax most of his muscles. Using artificial support or bones in the upper body as support allows him to relax and settle into position. Using muscles to support the rifle can cause it to move.

Natural point of aim. When the soldier first assumes his firing position, he orients his rifle in the general direction of his target. Then he adjusts his body to bring the rifle and sights exactly in line with the desired aiming point. When using proper support and consistent stock weld, the soldier should have his rifle and sights aligned naturally on the target. When this correct body-rifle-target alignment is achieved, the front sight post must be held on target, using muscular support and effort. As the rifle fires, the muscles tend to relax, causing the front sight to move away from the target toward the natural point of aim. Adjusting this point to the desired point of aim eliminates this movement. When multiple target exposures are expected (or a sector of fire must be covered), the soldier should adjust his natural point of aim to the center of the expected target exposure area (or center of sector).

Aiming. Focusing on the front sight post is a vital skill the firer must acquire during practice. Having mastered the task of holding the rifle steady, the soldier must align the rifle with the target in exactly the same way for each firing. The firer is the final judge as to where his eye is focused. The instructor/trainer emphasizes this point by having the firer focus on the target and then focus back on the front sight post. He checks the position of the firing eye to ensure it is in line with the rear sight aperture. He uses the M16 sighting device to see what the firer sees through the sights. (See Appendix C.)

Rifle sight alignment. Alignment of the rifle with the target is critical. It involves placing the tip of the front sight post in the center of the rear sight aperture. (Figure 3-4.) Any alignment error between the front and rear sights repeats itself for every 1/2 meter the bullet travels. For example, at the 25-meter line, any error in rifle alignment is multiplied 50 times. If the rifle is misaligned by 1/10 inch, it causes a target at 300 meters to be missed by 5 feet.

Figure 3-4. Correct sight alignment.

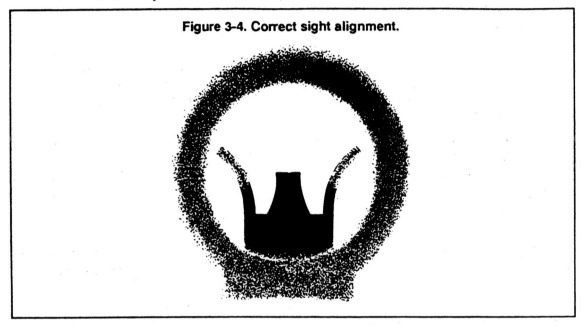

Focus of the eye. A proper firing position places the eye directly on line with the center of the rear sight. When the eye is focused on the front sight post, the natural ability of the eye to center objects in a circle and to seek the point of greatest light (center of the aperture) aid in providing correct sight alignment. For the average soldier firing at combat-type targets, the natural ability of the eye can accurately align the sights. Therefore, the firer can place the tip of the front sight post on the aiming point, but the eye must be focused on the tip of the front sight post. This causes the target to appear blurry, while the front sight post is seen clearly. Two reasons for focusing on the tip of the front sight post are:

- Only a minor aiming error should occur since the error reflects only as much as the soldier fails to determine the target center. A greater aiming error can result if the front sight post is blurry due to focusing on the target or other objects.

- Focusing on the tip of the front sight post aids the firer in maintaining proper sight alignment (Figure 3-4).

Sight picture. Once the soldier can correctly align his sights, he can obtain a sight picture. A correct sight picture has the target, front sight post, and rear sight aligned. The sight picture includes two basic elements: sight alignment and placement of the aiming point.

Placement of the aiming point varies, depending on the engagement range. For example, Figure 3-5 shows a silhouette at 250 meters—the aiming point is the center of mass, and the sights are in perfect alignment; this is a correct sight picture.

Figure 3-5. Correct sight picture.

A technique to obtain a good sight picture is the side aiming technique (Figure 3-6). It involves positioning the front sight post to the side of the target in line with the vertical center of mass, keeping the sights aligned. The front sight post is moved horizontally until the target is directly centered on the front sight post.

Figure 3-6. Side aiming technique.

Front sight. The front sight post is vital to proper firing and should be replaced when damaged. Two techniques that can be used are the carbide lamp and the burning plastic spoon. The post should be blackened anytime it is shiny since precise focusing on the tip of the front sight post cannot be done otherwise.

Aiming practice. Aiming practice is conducted before firing live rounds. During day firing, the soldier should practice sight alignment and placement of the aiming point. This can be done by using training aids such as the M15A1 aiming card and the Riddle sighting device. (See Appendix C.)

Breath Control. As the firer's skills improve and as timed or multiple targets are presented, he must learn to hold his breath at any part of the breathing cycle. Two types of breath control techniques are practiced during dry fire.

- The first is the technique used during zeroing (and when time is available to fire a shot) (Figure 3-7A. There is a moment of natural respiratory pause while breathing when most of the air has been exhaled from the lungs and before inhaling. Breathing should stop after most of the air has been exhaled during the normal breathing cycle. The shot must be fired before the soldier feels any discomfort.

- The second breath control technique is employed during rapid fire (short-exposure targets) (Figure 3-7B). Using this technique, the soldier holds his breath when he is about to squeeze the trigger.

The coach/trainer ensures that the firer uses two breathing techniques and understands them by instructing him to exaggerate his breathing. Also, the firer must be aware of the rifle's movement (while sighted on a target) as a result of breathing.

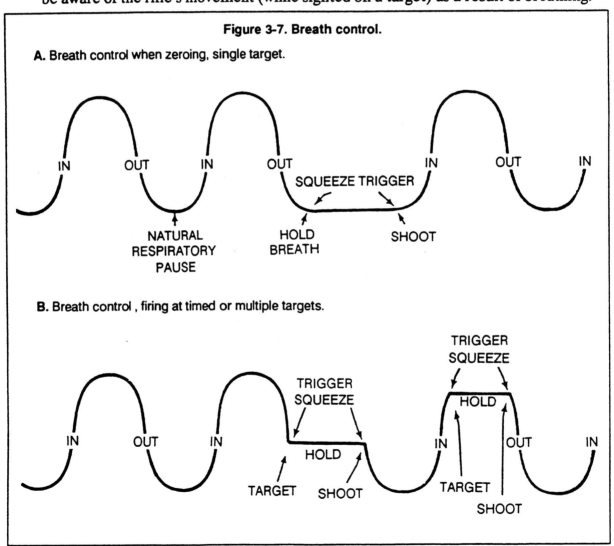

Figure 3-7. Breath control.

A. Breath control when zeroing, single target.

B. Breath control , firing at timed or multiple targets.

Trigger Squeeze. A novice firer can learn to place the rifle in a steady position and to correctly aim at the target if he follows basic principles. If the trigger is not properly squeezed, the rifle is misaligned with the target at the moment of firing.

Rifle movement. Trigger squeeze is important for two reasons:

- First, any sudden movement of the finger on the trigger can disturb the lay of the rifle and cause the shot to miss the target.

- Second, the precise instant of firing should be a surprise to the soldier.

The soldier's natural reflex to compensate for the noise and slight punch in the shoulder can cause him to miss the target if he knows the exact instant the rifle will fire. The soldier usually tenses his shoulders when expecting the rifle to fire, but it is difficult to detect since he does not realize he is flinching. When the hammer drops on a dummy round and does not fire, the soldier's natural reflexes demonstrate that he is improperly squeezing the trigger.

NOTE: See Appendix C for the Weaponeer and ball-and-dummy exercise. They are good training devices in detecting improper trigger squeeze.

Trigger finger. The trigger finger (index finger on the firing hand) is placed on the trigger between the first joint and the tip of the finger (not the extreme end) and is adjusted depending on hand size, grip, and so on. The trigger finger must squeeze the trigger to the rear so that the hammer falls without disturbing the lay of the rifle. When a live round is fired, it is difficult to see what affect trigger pull had on the lay of the rifle. Therefore, it is important to experiment with many finger positions during dry-fire training to ensure the hammer is falling with little disturbance to the aiming process.

As the firer's skills increase with practice, he needs less time spend on trigger squeeze. Novice firers can take five seconds to perform an adequate trigger squeeze, but, as skills improve, he can squeeze the trigger in a second or less. The proper trigger squeeze should start with slight pressure on the trigger during the initial aiming process. The firer applies more pressure after the front sight post is steady on the target and his is holding his breath.

The coach/trainer observes the trigger squeeze, emphasizes the correct procedure, and checks the firer's applied pressure. He places his finger on the trigger and has the firer squeeze the trigger by applying pressure to the coach/trainer's finger. The coach/trainer ensures that the firer squeezes straight to the rear on the trigger avoiding a left or right twisting movement. A steady position reduces disturbance of the rifle during trigger squeeze.

From an unsupported position, the firer experiences a greater wobble area than from a supported position. Wobble area is the movement of the front sight around the aiming point when the rifle is in the steadiest position. If the front sight strays from the target during the firing process, pressure on the trigger should be held constant and resumed as soon as sighting is corrected. The position must provide for the smallest possible wobble area. From a supported position, there should be minimal wobble area and little reason to detect movement. If movement of the rifle causes the front sight to leave the target, more practice is needed. The firer should never try to quickly squeeze the trigger while the sight is on the target. The best firing performance results when the trigger is squeezed continuously, and the rifle is fired without disturbing its lay.

FIRING POSITIONS

All firing positions are taught during basic rifle marksmanship training. During initial fundamental training, the basic firing positions are used. The other positions are added later in training to support tactical conditions.

Basic Firing Positions. Two firing positions are used during initial fundamental training: the individual supported fighting position and prone unsupported position. Both offer a stable platform for firing the rifle. They are also the positions used during basic record fire.

Supported fighting position. This position provides the most stable platform for engaging targets (Figure 3-8). Upon entering the position, the soldier adds or removes dirt, sandbags, or other supports to adjust for his height. He then faces the target, executes a half-face to his firing side, and leans forward until his chest is against the firing-hand corner of the position. He places the rifle handguard in a V formed by the thumb and fingers of his nonfiring hand, and rests the nonfiring hand on the material (sandbags or berm) to the front of the position. The soldier places the stock butt in the pocket of his firing shoulder and rests his firing elbow on the ground outside the position. (When prepared positions are not available, the prone supported position can be substituted.)

Figure 3-8. Supported fighting position.

Once the supported fighting position has been mastered, the firer should practice various unsupported positions to obtain the smallest possible wobble area during final aiming and hammer fall. The coach/trainer can check the steadiness of the position by observing movement at the forward part of the rifle, by looking through the M16 sighting device, or by checking to see that support is being used.

NOTE: The objective is to establish a steady position under various conditions. The ultimate performance of this task is in a combat environment. Although the firer must be positioned high enough to observe all targets, he must remain as low as possible to provide added protection from enemy fire.

Prone unsupported position. This firing position (Figure 3-9) offers another stable firing platform for engaging targets. To assume this position, the soldier faces his target, spreads his feet a comfortable distance apart, and drops to his knees. Using the butt of the rifle as a pivot, the firer rolls onto his nonfiring side, placing the nonfiring elbow close to the side of the magazine. He places the rifle butt in the pocket formed by the firing shoulder, grasps the pistol grip with his firing hand, and lowers the firing elbow to the ground. The rifle rests in the V formed by the thumb and fingers of the nonfiring hand. The soldier adjusts the position of his firing elbow until his shoulders are about level, and pulls back firmly on the rifle with both hands. To complete the position, he obtains a stock weld and relaxes, keeping his heels close to the ground.

Advanced Positions. After mastering the four marksmanship fundamentals in the

Figure 3-9. Prone unsupported position.

two basic firing positions, the soldier is taught the advanced positions. He is trained to assume different positions to adapt to the combat situation.

Alternate prone position (Figure 3-10). This position is an alternative to both prone supported and unsupported fighting positions, allowing the firer to cock his firing leg. The firer can assume a comfortable position while maintaining the same relationship between his body and the axis of the rifle. This position relaxes the stomach muscles and allows the firer to breathe naturally.

Kneeling supported position (Figure 3-11). This position allows the soldier to obtain the height necessary to better observe many target areas, taking advantage of available cover. Solid cover that can support any part of the body or rifle assists in firing accuracy.

Kneeling unsupported position (Figure 3-12). This position is assumed quickly, places the soldier high enough to see over small brush, and provides for a stable firing position. The nonfiring elbow should be pushed forward of the knee so that the upper arm is resting on a flat portion of the knee to provide stability. The trailing foot can be placed in a comfortable position.

Figure 3-10. Alternate prone position.

Figure 3-11. Kneeling supported position.

Figure 3-12. Kneeling unsupported position.

Standing position (Figure 3-13). To assume the standing position, the soldier faces his target, executes a facing movement to his firing side, and spreads his feet a comfortable distance apart. With his firing hand on the pistol grip and his nonfiring hand on either the upper handguard or the bottom of the magazine, the soldier places

Figure 3-13. Standing position.

the butt of the rifle in the pocket formed by his firing shoulder so that the sights are level with his eyes. The weight of the rifle is supported by the firing shoulder pocket and nonfiring hand. The soldier shifts his feet until he is aiming naturally at the target and his weight is evenly distributed on both feet. The standing position provides the least stability but could be needed for observing the target area since it can be assumed quickly while moving. Support for any portion of the body or rifle improves stability. More stability can be obtained by adjusting the ammunition pouch to support the nonfiring elbow, allowing the rifle magazine to rest in the nonfiring hand.

Modified Firing Positions. Once the basic firing skills have been mastered during initial training, the soldier should be encouraged to modify positions, to take advantage of available cover, to use anything that helps to steady the rifle, or to make any change that allows him to hit more combat targets. The position shown in Figure 3-14 uses sandbags to support the handguard and frees the nonfiring hand to be used on any part of the rifle to hold it steady.

NOTE: Modified positions can result in small zero changes due to shifting pressure and grip on the rifle.

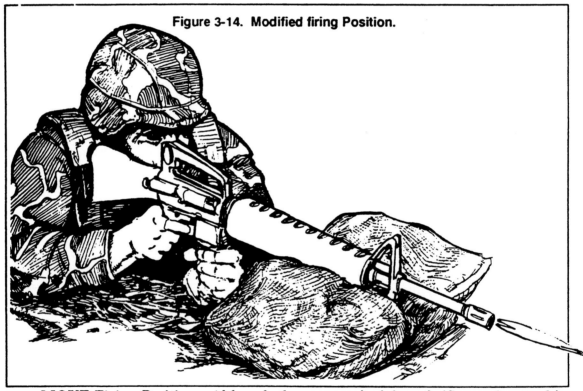

Figure 3-14. Modified firing Position.

MOUT Firing Positions. Although the same principles of rifle marksmanship apply, the selection and use of firing positions during MOUT requires some special considerations. Firing from around corners could require the soldier to fire from the opposite shoulder to avoid exposing himself to enemy fire.

The requirement for long-range observation can dictate that positions be occupied that are high above ground. Figure 3-15 shows a soldier firing over rooftops, exposing only the parts of his body necessary to engage a target. Figure 3-16 shows a soldier firing around obstacles. Figure 3-17 highlights the need to stay in the shadows while firing from windows, and the requirements for cover and rifle support.

Figure 3-15. Firing over rooftops.

Figure 3-16. Firing around obstacles.

Figure 3-17. Firing from windows.

Section III. DRY FIRE

Dry-fire exercises are conducted as they relate to each of the fundamentals of rifle marksmanship. The standard 25-meter zero targets (Figures 3-18 and 3-19) are mounted as illustrated, because they provide the consistent aiming point the soldier must use throughout preparatory marksmanship training.

CONDUCT OF DRY-FIRE TRAINING

A skilled instructor/trainer should supervise soldiers on dry-fire training. Once an explanation and demonstration are provided, soldiers should be allowed to work at their own pace, receiving assistance as needed. The peer coach-and-pupil technique can be effectively used during dry-fire training with the coach observing performance and offering suggestions. Several training aids are available to correctly conduct initial dry-fire training of the four fundamentals (Appendix C).

A supported firing position should be used to begin dry-fire training. Sandbags and chest-high support are used to effectively teach this position. While any targets at any range can be used, the primary aim point should be a standard silhouette zeroing target placed at a distance of 25 meters from the firing position. The other scaled-silhouette targets — slow fire and timed fire — are also excellent for advanced dry-fire training.

After the soldier understands and has practiced the four fundamentals, he proceeds to integrated dry-fire exercises. The objective of integrated dry fire is to master the four fundamentals of marksmanship in a complete firing environment. With proper dry-fire training, a soldier can assume a good, comfortable, steady firing position when he moves to the firing line. He must understand the aiming process, breath control is second nature, and correct trigger squeeze has been practiced many times. Also, by adding dummy ammunition to the soldier's magazine, other skills can be integrated into the dry-fire exercise to include practicing loading and unloading, reinforcing immediate-action drills, and using the dime (washer) exercise.

When correctly integrated, dry fire is an effective procedure to use before firing live bullets for grouping and zeroing, scaled silhouettes, field firing, or practice record fire. It can be used for remedial training or opportunity training, or as a primary training technique to maintain marksmanship proficiency.

PEER COACHING

Peer coaching is using two soldiers of equal firing proficiency and experience to assist (coach) each other during marksmanship training. Some problems exist with peer coaching. If the new soldier does not have adequate guidance, a "blind-leading-the-blind" situation results, which can lead to negative training and safety violations. However, when adequate instruction is provided, peer coaching can be helpful even in the IET environment. Since all soldiers in units have completed BRM, peer coaching should yield better results.

Benefits. The pairing of soldiers can enhance learning for both of them. The coach learns what to look for and what to check as he provides guidance to the firer. Communication between peers is different than communication between a firer and

Figure 3-18. The M16A1 and M16A2 zero targets.

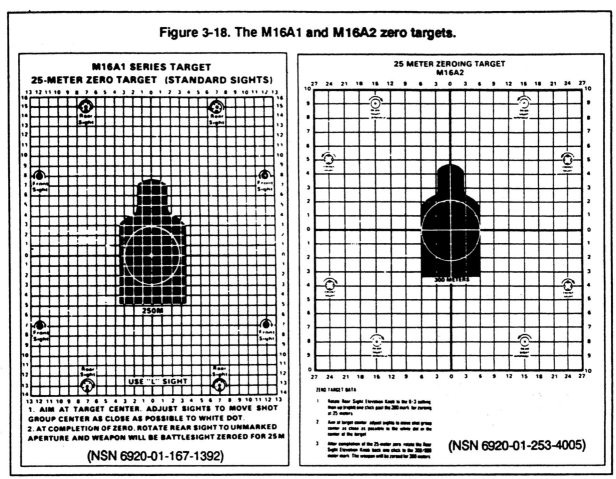

Figure 3-19. Zero target placed in the center of an E-type silhouette.

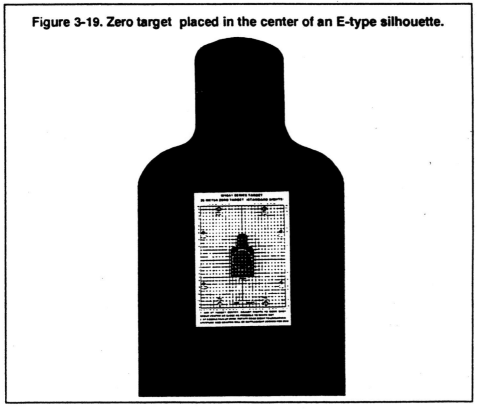

drill sergeant or senior NCO. Peers have the chance to ask simple questions and to discuss areas that are not understood. Pairing soldiers who have demonstrated good firing proficiency with those who have firing problems can improve the performance of problem firers

Duties. The peer coach assists the firer in obtaining a good position and in adjusting sandbags. He watches the firer — **not the target** — to see that the firer maintains a proper, relaxed, steady position; that he holds his breath before the final trigger squeeze; that he applies initial pressure to the trigger; and that no noticeable trigger jerk, flinch, eye blink, or other reaction can be observed in anticipating the rifle firing. The peer coach can use an M16 sighting device, allowing him to see what the firer sees through the sights. (Appendix C.)

The peer coach can load magazines, providing a chance to use ball and dummy. At other times, he could be required to observe the target area — for example, when field-fire targets are being engaged and the firer cannot see where he is missing targets. The peer coach can add to range safety procedures by helping safety personnel with preliminary rifle checks.

NOTE: When a peer coach is used during M16A1 live-fire exercises, a brass deflector should be attached to the rifle and eye protection should be worn.

CHECKLIST FOR THE COACH
The procedures to determine and eliminate rifle and firer deficiencies follows.

The coach checks to see that the —

- Rifle is cleared and defective parts have been replaced.
- Ammunition is clean, and the magazine is properly placed in the pouch.
- Sights are blackened and set correctly for long/short range.

The coach observes the firer to see that he —

- Uses the correct position and properly applies the steady-position elements.
- Properly loads the rifle.
- Obtains the correct sight alignment (with the aid of an M16 sighting device).
- Holds his breath correctly (by watching his back at times).
- Applies proper trigger squeeze; determines whether he flinches or jerks by watching his head, shoulders, trigger finger, and firing hand and arm.
- Is tense and nervous. If the firer is nervous, the coach has the firer breathe deeply several times to relax.

Supervisory personnel and peer coaches correct errors as they are detected. If many common errors are observed, it is appropriate to call the group together for more discussion and demonstration of proper procedures and to provide feedback.

POSITION OF THE COACH

The coach constantly checks and assists the firer in applying marksmanship fundamentals during firing. He observes the firer's position and his application of the steady position elements. The coach is valuable in checking factors the firer is unable to observe for himself and in preventing the firer from repeating errors.

During an exercise, the coach should be positioned where he can best observe the firer when he assumes position. He then moves to various points around the firer (sides and rear) to check the correctness of the firer's position. The coach requires the firer to make adjustments until the firer obtains a correct position.

When the coach is satisfied with the firing position, he assumes a coaching position alongside the firer. The coach usually assumes a position like that of the firer (Figure 3-20), which is on the firing side of the soldier.

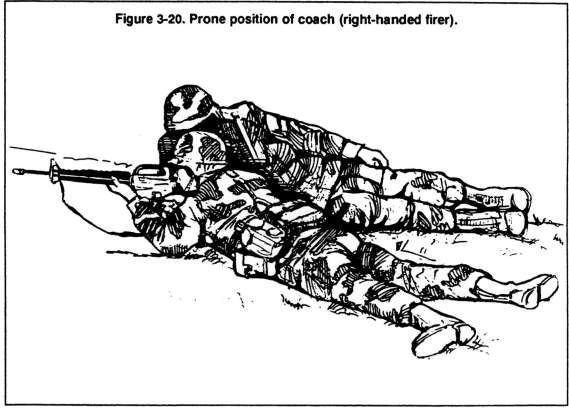

Figure 3-20. Prone position of coach (right-handed firer).

GROUPING

Shot grouping is a form of practice firing with two primary objectives: firing tight shot groups and consistently placing those groups in the same location. Shot grouping should be conducted between dry-fire training and zeroing. The initial live-fire training should be a grouping exercise with the purpose of practicing and refining marksmanship fundamentals. Since this is not a zeroing exercise, few sight changes are made. Grouping exercises can be conducted on a live-fire range that provides precise location of bullet hits and misses such as a 25-meter zeroing range or KD range.

CONCEPT OF ZEROING

The purpose of battlesight zeroing is to align the **fire control system** (sights) with the rifle barrel, considering the given ammunition ballistics. When this is accomplished correctly, the fire control and point of aim are point of impact at a **standard battlesight zero range** such as 250 (300) meters.

When a rifle is zeroed, the sights are adjusted so that bullet strike is the same as point of aim at some given range. A battlesight zero (250 meters, M16A1; 300 meters, M16A2) is the sight setting that provides the highest hit probability for most combat targets with minimum adjustment to the aiming point.

When standard zeroing procedures are followed, a rifle that is properly zeroed for one soldier is close to the zero for another soldier. When a straight line is drawn from target center to the tip of the front sight post and through the center of the rear aperture, it makes little difference whose eye is looking along this line. There are many subtle factors that result in differences among individual zeros; however, the similarity of individual zeros should be emphasized instead of the differences.

Most firers can fire with the same zeroed rifle if they are properly applying marksmanship fundamentals. If a soldier is having difficulty zeroing and the problem cannot be diagnosed, having a good firer zero the rifle could find the problem. When a soldier must fire another soldier's rifle without opportunity to verify the zero by firing—for example, picking up another man's rifle on the battlefield—it is closer to actual zero if the rifle sights are left unchanged. This information is useful in deciding initial sight settings and recording of zeros. All rifles in the arms room, even those not assigned, should have their sights aligned (zeroed) for battlesight zero.

There is no relationship between the specific sight setting a soldier uses on one rifle (his zero) to the sight setting he needs on another rifle. For example, a soldier could be required to move the rear sight of his assigned rifle 10 clicks left of center for zero, and the next rifle he is assigned could be adjusted 10 clicks right of center for zero. This is due to the inherent variability from rifle to rifle, which makes it essential that each soldier is assigned a permanent rifle on which all marksmanship training is conducted. Therefore, all newly assigned personnel should be required to fire their rifle for zero as soon as possible after assignment to the unit. The same rule must apply anytime a soldier is assigned a new rifle, a rifle is returned from DS or GS maintenance, or the zero is in question.

M16A1 STANDARD SIGHTS AND ZEROING

To battlesight zero the rifle, the soldier must understand sight adjustment procedures. The best possible zero is obtained by zeroing at actual range. Because facilities normally do not exist for zeroing at 250 meters, most zeroing is conducted at 25 meters. By pushing the rear sight forward so the L is exposed, the bullet crosses line of sight at 25 meters, reaches a maximum height above line of sight of about 11 inches at 225 meters, and crosses line of sight again at 375 meters (Figure 3-21).

To gain the many benefits associated with having bullets hit exactly where the rifle is aimed during 25-meter firing, the long-range sight is used on the zero range. Therefore, when bullets are adjusted to hit the same place the rifle is aimed at 25 meters, the bullet also hits where the rifle is aimed at 375 meters. After making this adjustment and flipping back to the short-range sight and aiming center of mass at a 42-meter target, the bullet crosses the line of sight at 42 meters and again at 250 meters as shown in Figure 3-22.

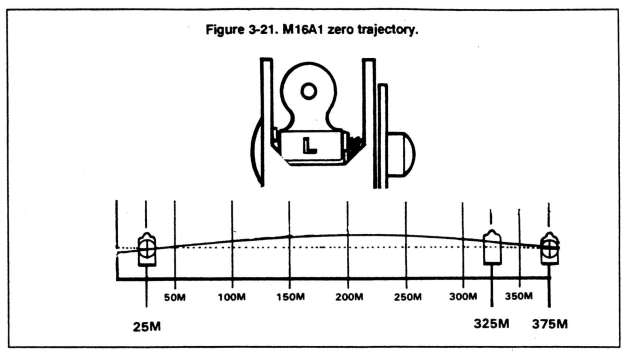

Figure 3-21. M16A1 zero trajectory.

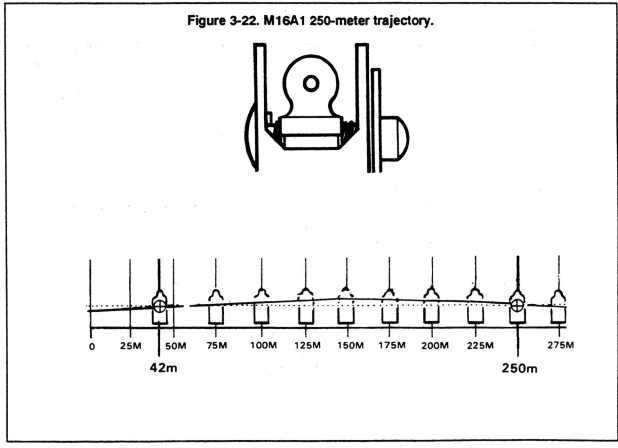

Figure 3-22. M16A1 250-meter trajectory.

Most combat targets are expected to be engaged in the ranges from 0 to 300 meters; therefore, the 250-meter battlesight zero is the setting that remains on the rifle. At 25 meters, the bullet is about 1 inch below line of sight, crossing line of sight at 42 meters. It reaches its highest point above the line of sight (about 5 inches) at a range of about 175 meters, crosses line of sight again at 250 meters, and is about 7 inches below line of sight at 300 meters. Targets can be hit out to a range of 300 meters with no adjustments to point of aim. (A somewhat higher hit probability results with minor adjustments to the aiming point.)

Sights. The sights are adjustable for both elevation and windage. Windage adjustments are made on the rear sight; elevation adjustments on the front sight.

Rear sight. The rear sight consists of two apertures and a windage drum with a spring-loaded detent (Figure 3-23). The aperture marked L is used for ranges beyond 300 meters, and the unmarked or short-range aperture is used for ranges up to 300 meters. Adjustments for windage are made by pressing in on the spring-loaded detent with a sharp instrument (or the tip of a cartridge) and rotating the windage drum in the desired direction of change (right or left) in the strike of the bullet.

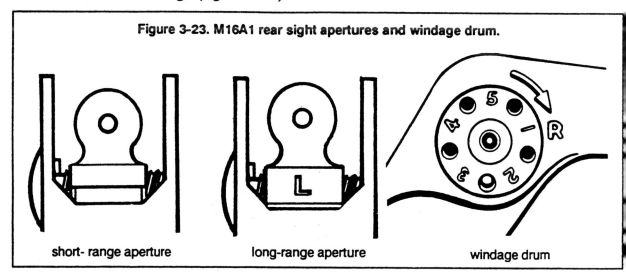

Figure 3-23. M16A1 rear sight apertures and windage drum.

| short- range aperture | long-range aperture | windage drum |

Front sight. The front sight consists of a round rotating sight post with a five-position, spring-loaded detent (Figure 3-24). Adjustments are made by using a sharp instrument (or the tip of a cartridge). To move the front sight post, the spring-loaded detent is depressed, and the post is rotated in the desired direction of change (up or down) in the strike of the bullet.

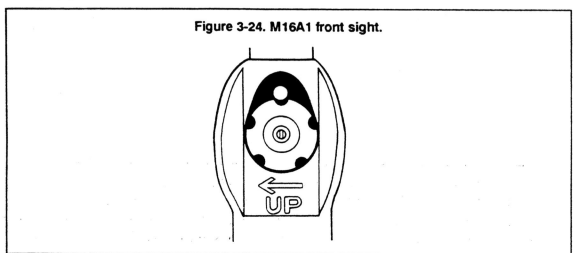

Figure 3-24. M16A1 front sight.

Sight Changes. To make sight changes, the firer first locates the center of his three-round shot group and then determines the distance between it and the desired location. An error in elevation is measured vertically, while a windage error is measured horizontally. When using standard zero targets or downrange feedback targets, sight adjustment guidance on the target is provided. (See Appendix F for the elevation and windage rule.)

To raise the strike of the bullet, the firer rotates the front sight post the desired number of clicks clockwise (in the direction of the arrow marked UP in Figure 3-24). Thus, the strike of the bullet is raised but the post is lowered. He reverses the direction of rotation to move the strike of the bullet down.

To move the strike of the bullet to the right, the windage drum is rotated the desired number of clicks clockwise (in the direction of the arrow marked R, Figure 3-23). The firer reverses the direction of rotation to move the strike of the bullet to the left.

NOTE: Before making any sight changes, the firer should make a serviceability check of the sights, looking for any bent, broken, or loose parts. The firer must also be able to consistently fire 4-cm shot groups.

M16A2 STANDARD SIGHTS AND ZEROING

When the soldier can consistently place three rounds within a 4-cm circle at 25 meters, regardless of group location, he is ready to zero his rifle.

The front and rear sights are set as follows:

Rear sight. The rear sight consists of two sight apertures, a windage knob, and an elevation knob (Figure 3-25).

Figure 3-25. M16A2 rear sight.

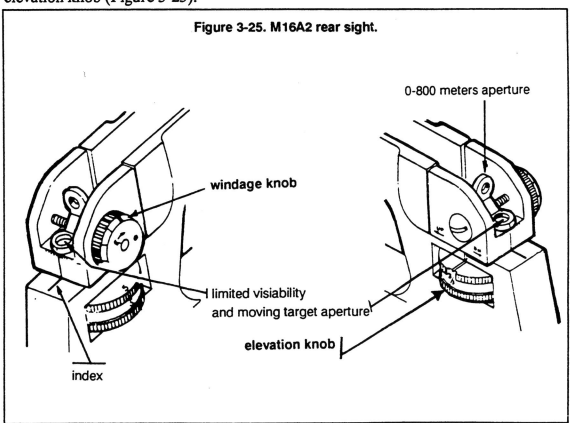

0-800 meters aperture

windage knob

limited visiability and moving target aperture

elevation knob

index

The larger aperture, marked 0-2, is used for moving target engagement and during limited visibility. The unmarked aperture is used for normal firing situations, zeroing, and with the elevation knob for target distances up to 800 meters. The unmarked aperture is used to establish the battlesight zero.

After the elevation knob is set, adjustments for elevation are made by moving the front sight post up or down to complete zeroing the rifle. Adjustments for windage are made by turning the windage knob.

The rear windage knob start point is when the index mark on the 0-2 sight is aligned with the rear sight base index (Figure 3-26).

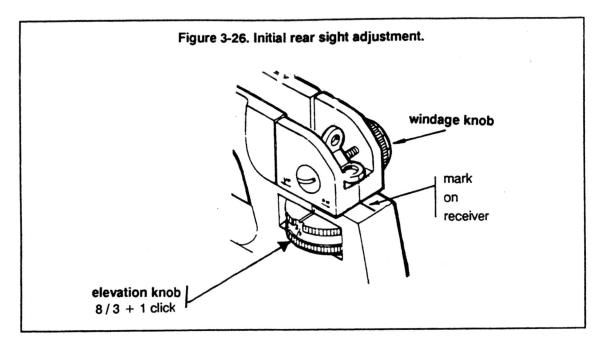

Figure 3-26. Initial rear sight adjustment.

windage knob

mark
on
receiver

elevation knob
8 / 3 + 1 click

Front sight. The front sight is adjusted the same as the front sight of the M16A1. It consists of a square, rotating sight post with a four-position, spring-loaded detent (Figure 3-27). Adjustments are made by using a sharp instrument or the tip of a cartridge. To raise or lower the front sight post, the spring-loaded detent is depressed, and the post is rotated in the desired direction of change. (Figure 3-28).

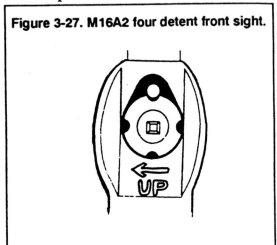

Figure 3-27. M16A2 four detent front sight.

UP

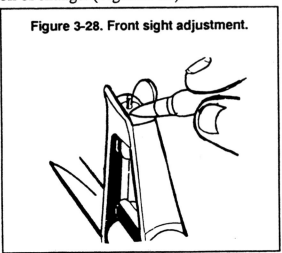

Figure 3-28. Front sight adjustment.

DOWNRANGE FEEDBACK TRAINING

The term downrange feedback describes any training method that provides precise knowledge of bullet strike (exactly where bullets hit or miss the intended target) at ranges beyond 25 meters. The soldier gains confidence in his firing abilities by knowing what happens to bullets at range. The inclusion of downrange feedback during the initial learning process and during refresher training improves the soldier's firing proficiency and record fire scores. Downrange feedback can be incorporated into any part of a unit's marksmanship program. However, an ideal sequence is to conduct downrange feedback following 25-meter firing and before firing on the field fire range. (See Appendix G.)

The use of a KD firing range is an excellent way of providing downrange feedback. Also a good way to obtain downrange feedback is to modify existing field fire ranges by constructing target-holding frames, which requires the soldier to walk from the firing line to the target to locate bullet strike.

Units can design their own downrange feedback training to accommodate available facilities. Any silhouette target with a backing large enough to catch all bullet misses can be set up at any range. For example, it would be ideal if the confirmation of weapon zero could be conducted at the actual zero range of 250 meters/300 meters.

FIELD FIRE TRAINING

Field fire training provides the transition from unstressed slow firing at known-distance/feedback targets to engaging fleeting combat-type pop-up silhouettes. Two basic types of field firing exercises are single-target and multiple-target engagements, which use 75-, 175-, and 300-meter targets. Once the soldier has developed the unstressed firing skills necessary to hit single KD targets, he must learn to detect and quickly engage combat-type targets at various ranges. Time standards are provided during this instruction to add stress and to simulate the short exposure times of combat targets. The soldier must, therefore, detect, acquire, and engage the target before the exposure ends. During field fire training, the firer learns to quickly detect and apply the fundamentals at the same time. (See Appendix G.)

PRACTICE RECORD FIRE

Practice record fire is a training exercise designed to progressively develop and refine the soldiers combat firing skills. During this exercise, the soldier is exposed to a more difficult course of fire with increased time stress to include single and multiple target engagements at six distances ranging from 50 to 300 meters. This exercise also provides the opportunity to practice and demonstrate skills learned during target detection. To perform well, a soldier must integrate all the tasks learned from previous training. When firing exercises are properly organized, conducted, and critiqued, the soldier gains knowledge and confidence in his firing performance. Through close observation, coaching, and critiquing, instructors/trainers can base remedial training on specific needs. (See Appendix G.)

RECORD FIRE

Qualification ratings and first-time GO rates are important during record fire, if properly used. They provide goals for the soldier and aid the commander in identifying the quality of his training. This should be considered in the assignment of priorities, instructor personnel, and obtaining valuable training resources. The objective of record firing is to access and confirm the individual proficiency of firers and the effectiveness of the training program. (See Appendix A for information on unit training and Appendix G for detailed information on record fire.)

CHAPTER 4

Combat Fire Techniques

The test of a soldier's training is applying the fundamentals of marksmanship and firing skills in combat. The marksmanship skills mastered during training, practice, and record fire exercises must be applied to many combat situations (attack, assault, ambush, MOUT). Although these situations present problems, only two modifications of the basic techniques and fundamentals are necessary (see Chapter 3): changes to the rate of fire and alterations in weapon/target alignment. The necessary changes are significant and must be thoroughly taught and practiced before discussing live-fire exercises.

NOTE: For tactical applications of fire see FM 7-8.

Section I. SUPPRESSIVE FIRE

In many tactical situations, combat rifle fire will be directed to suppress enemy personnel or weapons positions. Rifle fire, which is precisely aimed at a definite point or area target, is suppressive fire. Some situations may require a soldier to place suppressive fire into a wide area such as a wood line, hedgerow, or small building. While at other times, the target may be a bunker or window. Suppressive fire is used to control the enemy and the area he occupies. Suppressive fire is employed to kill the enemy or to prevent him from observing the battlefield or effectively using his weapons. When a sustained volume of accurate suppressive fire is placed on enemy locations to contain him, it can be effective even though he cannot be seen. When the enemy is effectively pinned down behind cover, this reduces his ability to deliver fire and allows friendly forces to move.

NATURE OF THE TARGET
Many soldiers have difficulty delivering effective suppressive fire when they cannot see a definite target. They must fire at likely locations or in a general area where the enemy is known to exist. Even though definite targets cannot be seen, most suppressive fire should be well aimed. Figure 4-1, page 4-2, shows a landscape target suitable for suppressive fire training. When this type target is used, trainers must develop a firing program to include areas of engagement and designated target areas that will be credited as sustained effective suppressive fire. At 25 meters, this target provides the firer with an area to suppress without definite targets to engage.

POINT OF AIM
Suppressive fire should be well-aimed, sustained, semiautomatic fire. Although lacking a definite target, the soldier must be taught to control and accurately deliver fire within the limits of the suppressed area. The sights are used as when engaging a point-type target—with the front sight post placed so that each shot impacts within the desired area (window, firing portal, tree line).

Figure 4-1. Landscape target.

RATE OF FIRE

During most phases of live fire (grouping, zeroing, qualifying), shots are delivered using the slow semiautomatic rate of fire (one round every 3 to 10 seconds). During training, this allows for a slow and precise application of the fundamentals. Successful suppressive fire requires that a faster but sustained rate of fire be used. Sometimes firing full automatic bursts (13 rounds per second) for a few seconds may be necessary to gain initial fire superiority. Rapid semiautomatic fire (one round every one or two seconds) allows the firer to sustain a large volume of accurate fire while conserving ammunition. The tactical situation dictates the most useful rate of fire, but the following must be considered:

Applying Fundamentals. As the stress of combat increases, some soldiers may fail to apply the fundamentals of marksmanship. This factor contributes to soldiers firing less accurately and without obtaining the intended results. While some modifications are appropriate, the basic fundamentals should be applied and emphasized regardless of the rate of fire or combat stress.

Making Rapid Magazine Changes. One of the keys to sustained suppressive fire is rapidly reloading the rifle. Rapid magazine changes must be correctly taught and practiced during dry-fire and live-fire exercises until the soldier becomes proficient. Small-unit training exercises must be conducted so that soldiers who are providing suppressive fire practice magazine changes that are staggered. Firing is, therefore, controlled and coordinated so that a continuous volume of accurate suppressive fire is delivered to the target area.

Conserving Ammunition. Soldiers must be taught to make each round count. Automatic fire should be used sparingly and only to gain initial fire superiority. Depending on the tactical situation, the rate of fire should be adjusted so that a minimum number of rounds are expended. Accurate fire conserves ammunition, while preventing the enemy from placing effective fire on friendly positions.

Section II. RAPID SEMIAUTOMATIC FIRE

Rapid semiautomatic fire delivers a large volume of accurate fire into a target or target area. Increases in speed and volume should be sought only after the soldier has demonstrated expertise and accuracy during slow semiautomatic fire. The rapid application of the four fundamentals will result in a well-aimed shot every one or two seconds. This technique of fire allows a unit to place the most effective volume of fire in a target area while conserving ammunition. It is the most accurate means of delivering suppressive fire.

EFFECTIVENESS OF RAPID FIRE

When a soldier uses rapid semiautomatic fire, he is sacrificing accuracy to deliver a greater volume of fire. The difference in accuracy between slow and rapid semiautomatic fire diminishes with proper training and repeated practice. Training and practice improve the soldier's marksmanship skills to the point that accuracy differences become minimal. There is little difference in the volume of effective fire that would be delivered by units using much less accurate automatic fire.

NOTE: Learning rapid fire techniques also improves the soldier's response time to short-exposure, multiple, and moving targets.

MODIFICATIONS FOR RAPID FIRE

Trainers must consider the impact of the increased rate of fire on the soldier's ability to properly apply the fundamentals of marksmanship and other combat firing skills. These fundamentals/skills include:

Immediate Action. To maintain an increased rate of suppressive fire, immediate action must be applied quickly. The firer must identify the problem and correct the stoppage immediately. Repeated dry-fire practice, using blanks or dummy rounds, followed by live-fire training and evaluation ensures that soldiers can rapidly apply immediate action while other soldiers initiate fire.

Marksmanship Fundamentals. The four fundamentals are used when firing in the rapid semiautomatic mode. The following differences apply:

Steady position. Good support improves accuracy and reduces recovery time between shots. somewhat tighter grip on the handguards assists in recovery time and in rapidly shifting or distributing fire to subsequent targets. When possible, the rifle should pivot at the point where the nonfiring hand meets the support. The soldier should avoid changing the position of the nonfiring hand on the support, because it is awkward and time-consuming when rapidly firing a series of shots.

Aiming. The aiming process does not change during rapid semiautomatic fire. The firer's head remains on the stock, his firing eye is aligned with the rear aperture, and his focus is on the front sight post.

Breath control. Breath control must be modified because the soldier does not have time to take a complete breath between shots. He must hold his breath at some point in the firing process and take shallow breaths between shots.

Trigger squeeze. To maintain the desired rate of fire, the soldier has only a short period to squeeze the trigger (one well-aimed shot every one or two seconds).

The firer must cause the rifle to fire in a period of about one-half of a second or less and still not anticipate the precise instant of firing. Rapid semiautomatic trigger squeeze is difficult to master. It is important that initial trigger pressure be applied as soon as a target is identified and while the front sight post is being brought to the desired point of aim. When the post reaches the point of aim, final pressure must be applied to cause the rifle to fire almost at once. This added pressure, or final trigger squeeze, must be applied without disturbing the lay of the rifle.

Repeated dry-fire training, using the Weaponeer device, and live-fire practice ensure the soldier can squeeze the trigger and maintain a rapid rate of fire consistently and accurately.

NOTE: When presented with multiple targets, the soldier may fire the first round, release pressure on the trigger to reset the sear, then reapply more pressure to fire the next shot. This technique eliminates the time used in releasing all the trigger pressure. It allows the firer to rapidly deliver subsequent rounds. Training and practice sessions are required for soldiers to become proficient in the technique of rapid trigger squeeze.

Magazine Changes. Rapid magazine changes are an integral part of sustaining rapid semiautomatic suppressive fire. Soldiers must quickly reload their rifles and resume accurate firing.

Magazine handling. Most units establish the soldier's basic load of ammunition and loaded magazines. The number of magazines vary based on the mission and tactical situation. During combat, some magazines are lost, but it is the soldier's responsiblility to keep this loss to a minimum. While training a soldier to reload his magazines, the trainer must emphasize the need to account for these magazines.

The sequence for magazine handling during rapid changes is illustrated for right- and left-handed firers in Figure 4-2.

Rifle loading. Removing a magazine from the firing side ammunition pouch is the same for both right- and left-handed firers. Empty magazines must be removed from the rifle before performing the following.

To remove a magazine from the pouch, the magazine is grasped on the long edge with the thumb, and the first and second fingers are placed on the short edge.

The magazine is withdrawn from the ammunition pouch, and the arm is extended forward, rotating the hand and wrist so that the magazine is in position (open end up and long edge to the rear) to load into the rifle. It is loaded into the rifle by inserting the magazine straight up into the magazine well until it is seated. The base of the magazine is tapped with the heel of the hand to ensure the magazine is fully seated.

Removing a magazine from the nonfiring side of the ammunition pouch requires the firer to support the rifle with his firing hand. His nonfiring hand grasps the magazine and loads it into the rifle.

Rapid magazine changing. Training and repeated practice in this procedure improves soldier proficiency. The firer does not move the selector lever to SAFE during a rapid magazine change, but he must maintain a safe posture during the change.

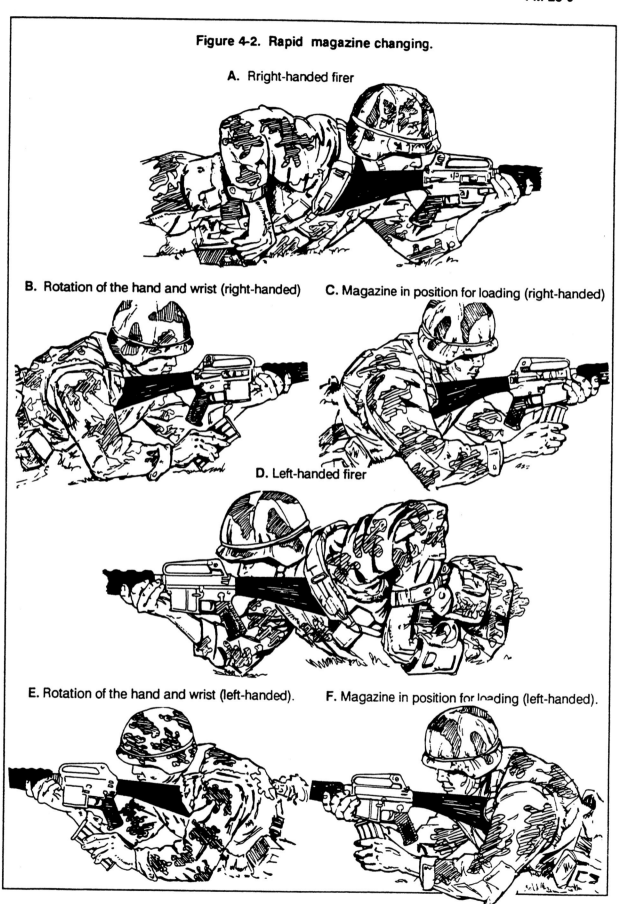

Figure 4-2. Rapid magazine changing.

A. Rright-handed firer

B. Rotation of the hand and wrist (right-handed)

C. Magazine in position for loading (right-handed)

D. Left-handed firer

E. Rotation of the hand and wrist (left-handed).

F. Magazine in position for loading (left-handed).

The following is a step-by-step sequence for rapid magazine changing.

- *Right-handed firer.* Remove the index finger from the trigger and depress the magazine catch button while keeping a secure grip on the rifle with the nonfiring hand (Figure 4-3). Release the pistol grip, grasp and remove the empty magazine with the right (firing) hand, and secure it. Grasp the loaded magazine with the right hand (rounds up and forward). Insert the loaded magazine into the magazine well and tap upward with the palm of the right hand. This ensures that the magazine is fully seated and locked into the rifle. Depress the upper half of the bolt catch with the fingers of the right hand. This allows the bolt to go forward, chambering the first round. If necessary, use the right hand to tap the forward assist to fully chamber the first round. Return the right hand to its original firing position on the pistol grip. Return the index finger to the trigger.

Figure 4-3. Magazine release catch button being depressed (right-handed firer).

- *Left-handed firer.* Remove the index finger from the trigger and release the pistol grip. Depress the magazine catch button with the index finger of the left (firing) hand. Remove the empty magazine with the left hand and secure it. Grasp the loaded magazine with the left hand (rounds up, bullets forward). Insert the loaded magazine into the magazine well and tap upward with the palm of the left hand. This ensures that the magazine is fully seated and locked into the rifle. Depress the upper half of the bolt catch with a finger of the left hand. This allows the bolt to go forward, chamberng the first round. If necessary, use the right hand to tap the forward assist to fully chamber the first round. Return the left hand to its original firing position on the pistol grip. Return the index finger to the trigger. The firer must maintain a safe posture during the change.

When loading from the nonfiring side, the previous steps are followed with with this exception: the loaded magazine is secured and inserted into the magazine well with the nonfiring hand. The firing hand supports the rifle at the pistol grip. After the magazine is inserted, the firer should shift the rifle's weight to his nonfiring hand and continue with the recommended sequence.

RAPID-FIRE TRAINING

Soldiers should be well trained in all aspects of slow semiautomatic firing before attempting any rapid-fire training. Those who display a lack of knowledge of the fundamental skills should not advance to rapid semiautomatic training until these skills are learned. Initial training should focus on the modifications to the fundamentals and other basic combat skills necessary during rapid semiautomatic firing.

Dry-Fire Exercises. Repeated dry-fire exercises are the most efficient means available to ensure soldiers can apply modifications to the fundamentals. Multiple dry-fire exercises are needed, emphasizing a rapid shift in position and point of aim, followed by breath control and fast trigger squeeze. Blanks or dummy rounds may be used to train rapid magazine changes and the application of immediate action. The soldier should display knowledge and skill during these dry-fire exercises before attempting live fire.

Live-Fire Exercises. There are two types of live-fire exercises.

Individual. Emphasis is on each soldier maintaining a heavy volume of accurate fire. Weapon down time (during immediate action and rapid magazine changes) is kept to a minimum. Firing should begin at shorter ranges, progressing to longer ranges as soldiers display increased proficiency. Exposure or engagement times are shortened and the number of rounds increased to simulate the need for a heavy volume of fire. Downrange feedback is necessary to determine accuracy of fire.

Unit. Rapid semiautomatic fire should be the primary means of delivering fire during a unit LFX. It is the most accurate technique of placing a large volume of fire on poorly defined targets or target areas. Emphasis should be on staggered rapid magazine changes, maintaining a continuous volume of fire and conserving ammunition.

Section III. AUTOMATIC FIRE

Automatic fire delivers the maximum amount of rounds into a target area. It should be trained only after the soldier has demonstrated expertise during slow and rapid semiautomatic fire. Automatic fire involves the rapid application of the four fundamentals while delivering from 3 to 13 rounds per second into a designated area. This technique of fire allows a unit to place the most fire in a target area (when conserving ammunition is not a consideration). It is a specialized technique of delivering suppressive fire and may not apply to most combat engagements. The M16A1 rifle has a full automatic setting. (The M16A2 uses a three-round burst capability.) Soldiers must be taught the advantages and disadvantages of automatic firing so they know when it should be used. Without this knowledge, in a life-threatening situation the soldier will tend to switch to the automatic/burst mode. This fire can be effective in some situations. It is vital for the unit to train and practice the appropriate use of automatic fire.

EFFECTIVENESS OF AUTOMATIC FIRE

Automatic fire is inherently less accurate than semiautomatic fire. The first automatic shot fired may be on target, but recoil and high-cyclic rate of fire often combine to place subsequent rounds far from the desired point of impact. Even controlled (three-round burst) automatic fire may place only one round on the target. Because of these inaccuracies, it is difficult to evaluate the effectiveness of automatic fire, and even more difficult to establish absolute guidelines for its use.

Closely spaced multiple targets, appearing at the same time at 50 meters or closer, may be engaged effectively with automatic/burst fire. More widely spaced targets appearing at greater distances should be engaged with semiautomatic fire.

The M16A1 and M16A2 rifles should normally be employed in the semiautomatic mode. Depending on the tactical situation, the following conditions would be factors against the use of automatic fire:

- Ammunition is in short supply or resupply may be difficult.

- Single targets are being engaged.

- Widely spaced multiple targets are being engaged.

- The distance to the target is beyond 50 meters.

- The effect of bullets on the target cannot be observed.

- Artificial support is not available.

- Targets may be effectively engaged using semiautomatic fire.

In some combat situations, the use of automatic fire can improve survivability and enhance mission accomplishment. Clearing buildings, final assaults, FPF, and ambushes may require the limited use of automatic fire. Depending on the tactical situation, the following conditions may favor the use of automatic fire:

- Enough available ammunition. Problems are not anticipated with resupply.

- Closely spaced multiple targets appear at 50 meters or less.

- Maximum fire is immediately required at an area target.

- Tracers or some other means can be used to observe the effect of bullets on the target.

- Leaders can maintain adequate control over rifles firing on automatic.

- Good artificial support is available.

- The initial sound of gunfire disperses closely spaced targets.

Trainers must ensure soldiers understand the capabilities and limitations of automatic fire. They must know when it should and should not be used.

MODIFICATIONS FOR AUTOMATIC FIRE POSITIONS

Trainers must consider the impact of the greatly increased rate of fire on the soldier's ability to properly apply the fundamentals of marksmanship and other combat firing skills. These fundamentals/skills include:

Immediate Action. To maintain automatic fire, immediate action must be applied quickly. The firer must identify the problem and correct it immediately. Repeated dry-fire practice, using blanks or dummy rounds, followed by live-fire training and evaluation ensures that soldiers can rapidly apply immediate action.

Marksmanship Fundamentals. The four fundamentals are used when firing in the automatic mode. The following differences apply:

Steady position (Figure 4-4). Maximum use of available artificial support is necessary during automatic fire. The rifle should be gripped more firmly and pulled into the shoulder more securely than when firing in the semiautomatic mode. This support and increased grip help to offset the progressive displacement of weapon/target alignment caused by recoil. To provide maximum stability, prone and supported positions are best. One possible modification involves forming a 5-inch loop with the

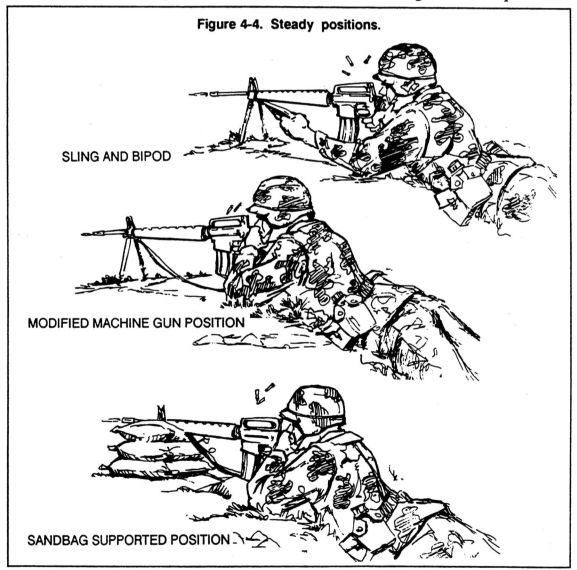

Figure 4-4. Steady positions.

SLING AND BIPOD

MODIFIED MACHINE GUN POSITION

SANDBAG SUPPORTED POSITION

sling at the upper sling swivel, grasping this loop with the nonfiring hand, and pulling down and to the rear while firing. Another modification involves grasping the small of the stock with the nonfiring hand, and applying pressure down and to the rear while firing. If a bipod is not available, sandbags may be used to support the rifle. The nonfiring hand may be positioned on the rifle wherever it provides the most stability and flexibility. The goal is to maintain weapon stability and minimize recoil.

Aiming. The aiming process does not change during automatic fire. The firer's head remains on the stock, his firing eye stays aligned with the rear sight aperture, and his focus is on the front sight post. Although recoil may disrupt this process, the firer must try to apply the aiming techniques throughout recoil.

Breath control. Breath control must be modified because the firer will not have the time to breathe between shots. He must hold his breath for each burst and adapt his breathing cycle, taking breaths between bursts.

Trigger squeeze. Training and repeated dry-fire practice will aid the soldier in applying proper trigger squeeze during automatic firing. Live-fire exercises will enable him to improve this skill.

NOTE: The trigger is not slapped or jerked. It is squeezed and pressure is quickly released.

- **M16A1.** Trigger squeeze is applied in the normal manner up to the instant the rifle fires. Because three-round bursts are the most effective rate of fire, pressure on the trigger should be released as soon as possible. The index finger should remain on the trigger, but a quick release of pressure is necessary to prevent an excessive amount of rounds from being fired in one burst. With much dry-fire practice, the soldier can become proficient at delivering three-round bursts with the squeeze/release technique.

- **M16A2.** Trigger squeeze is applied in the normal manner up to the instant the rifle fires. Using the burst-mode, the firer holds the trigger to the rear until three rounds are fired. He then releases pressure on the trigger until it resets, then reapplies pressure for the next three-round burst.

NOTE: Depending on the position of the burst cam when the selector is moved to the burst mode, the rifle may fire one, two, or three rounds when the trigger is held to the rear the first time. If the rifle fires only one or two rounds, the firer must quickly release pressure on the trigger and squeeze again, holding it to the rear until a three-round burst is completed.

Magazine Changes. Rapid magazine changes are vital in maintaining automatic fire. (See SECTION II. RAPID SEMIAUTOMATIC FIRE, Magazine Handling, for detailed information on rapid magazine changes.)

TRAINING OF AUTOMATIC FIRE TECHNIQUES

Soldiers should be well trained in all aspects of slow semiautomatic firing before attempting any automatic training. Those who display a lack of knowledge of the fundamental skills should not advance to automatic fire training until these skills are learned. Initial training should focus on the modifications to the fundamentals and other basic combat skills necessary during automatic firing.

Dry-Fire Exercises. Repeated dry-fire exercises are the most efficient means available to ensure soldiers can apply these modifications. Multiple dry-fire exercises are needed, emphasizing a stable position and point of aim, followed by breath control and the appropriate trigger squeeze. Blanks or dummy rounds may be used to train trigger squeeze, rapid magazine changes, and application of immediate action. The soldier should display knowledge and skill during these exercises before attempting live fire.

Live-Fire Exercises. There are two types of live-fire exercises.

Individual. Emphasis is on each individual maintaining a heavy volume of fire. Weapon down time (during immediate action and rapid magazine changes) is held to a minimum. Firing can begin at 25 meters, progressing to 50 meters as soldiers display increased proficiency. Exposure or engagement times, as well as ranges, are varied to best simulate the need for a heavy volume of fire. Downrange feedback is necessary to determine effectiveness of fire. The course of fire should allow the soldier to decide whether he should engage a given target or area with automatic or semiautomatic fire.

A soldier's zero during automatic fire may be different than his semiautomatic (battlesight) zero. This is due to the tendency of the lightweight M16 barrel to respond to external pressure such as the bipod or pulling on the sling. However, it is recommended that the battlesight zero be retained on the rifle and holdoff used to place automatic fire on the target. This holdoff training requires downrange feedback and should be conducted before other live-fire exercises.

The soldier can begin by loading and firing one round from an automatic fire position. Three of these rounds, treated as a single group, can establish where the first shot of a three-round burst will probably strike. Loading and firing two rounds simulates the dispersion of the second shot of a three-round burst. Finally, several three-round bursts should be fired to refine any necessary holdoff to center these larger groups on the desired point of impact.

Unit. Unit LFXs should include the careful use of automatic fire. Emphasis should be on staggered rapid magazine changes, maintaining a continuous volume of heavy fire, and conserving ammunition.

Section IV. QUICK FIRE

The two main techniques of directing fire with a rifle are to aim using the sights; and to use weapon alignment, instinct, bullet strike, or tracers to direct the fire. The preferred technique is to use the sights, but sometimes quick reflex action is needed to survive. Quick fire is a technique used to deliver fast, effective fire on surprise personnel targets at close ranges (25 meters or less). Quick-fire procedures have also been referred to as "instinct firing" or "quick kill."

EFFECTIVENESS OF QUICK FIRE

Quick-fire techniques are appropriate for soldiers who are presented with close, suddenly appearing, surprise enemy targets; or when close engagement is imminent. Fire may be delivered in the SEMIAUTO or BURST/AUTO mode. For example, a point man in a patrol may carry the weapon on BURST/AUTO. This may also be required when clearing a room or bunker. Initial training should be in the SEMI mode. Two techniques of delivering quick fire are —

Aimed. When presented with a target, the soldier brings the rifle up to his shoulder and quickly fires a single shot. His firing eye looks through or just over the rear sight aperture, and he uses the front sight post to aim at the target (Figure 4-5). Using this technique, a target at 25 meters or less may be accurately engaged in one second or less.

Pointed. When presented with a target, the soldier keeps the rifle at his side and quickly fires a single shot or burst. He keeps both eyes open and uses his instinct and peripheral vision to line up the rifle with the target (Figure 4-6). Using this technique, a target at 15 meters or less may be engaged in less than one second.

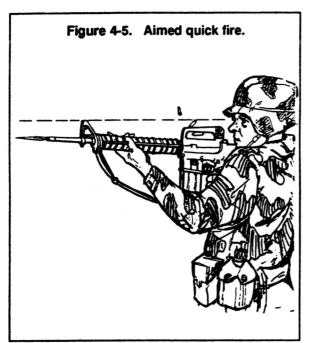

Figure 4-5. Aimed quick fire.

Figure 4-6. Pointed quick fire.

The difference in speed of delivery between these two techniques is small. Pointed quick fire can be used to fire a shot about one-tenth of a second faster than aimed quick fire. The difference in accuracy, however, is more pronounced. A soldier well trained in pointed quick fire can hit an E-type silhouette target at 15 meters, although the shot may strike anywhere on the target. A soldier well trained in aimed quick fire can hit an E-type silhouette target at 25 meters, with the shot or burst striking 5 inches from the center of mass.

The key to the successful employment of either technique is practice. Both pointed and aimed quick fire must be repeatedly practiced during dry-fire training. Live-fire exercises provide further skill enhancement and illustrate the difference in accuracy between the two techniques. Tactical considerations dictate which technique is most effective in a given situation, and when single shot versus burst fire is used.

Pointed and aimed quick fire should be used only when a target cannot be engaged fast enough using the sights in a normal manner. These techniques should be limited to targets appearing at 25 meters or less.

MODIFICATIONS FOR QUICK- FIRE TECHNIQUES

Quick-fire techniques require major modifications to the four fundamentals of marksmanship. These modifications represent a significant departure from the normal applications of the four fundamentals. Initial training in these differences, followed by repeated dry-fire exercises, will be necessary to prepare the soldier for live fire.

Steady Position. The quickness of shot delivery prevents the soldier from assuming a stable firing position. He must fire from his present position when the target appears. If the soldier is moving, he must stop. Adjustments for stability and support cannot be made before the round being fired.

Aimed. The butt of the rifle is pulled into the pocket of the shoulder as the cheek comes in contact with the stock. Both hands firmly grip the rifle, applying rearward pressure. The firing eye looks through or just over the rear sight aperture (Figure 4-5, page 4-12). The firer's sight is in focus and placed on the target.

Pointed. The rifle is pulled into the soldier's side and both hands firmly grip the rifle, applying rearward pressure (Figure 4-6, page 4-12).

Aiming. This fundamental must be highly modified because the soldier may not have time to look through the rear sight, find the front sight, and align it with the target.

Aimed. The soldier's initial focus is on the target. As the rifle is brought up, the firing eye looks through or just over the rear sight aperture at the target. Using his peripheral vision, the soldier locates the front sight post and brings it to the center of the target. When the front sight post is in focus, the shot is fired. Focus remains on the front sight post throughout the aiming process.

Pointed. The soldier's focus is placed on the center or slightly below the center of the target as the rifle is aligned with it and is fired. The soldier's instinctive pointing ability and peripheral vision are used to aid in proper alignment.

NOTE: When using either aiming technique, bullets may tend to impact above the desired location. Repeated live-fire practice is necessary to determine the best aim point on the target or the best focus. Such practice should begin with the soldier using a center mass arms/focus.

Breath Control. This fundamental has little application to the first shot of quick fire. The round must be fired before a conscious decision can be made about breathing. If subsequent shots are necessary, breathing must not interfere with the necessity to fire quickly. When possible, use short, shallow breaths.

Trigger Squeeze. Initial pressure is applied as weapon alignment is moved toward the target. Trigger squeeze is exerted so that when weapon/target alignment is achieved, the round is fired at once. The soldier requires much training and practice to perfect this rapid squeezing of the trigger.

TRAINING OF QUICK- FIRE TECHNIQUES

Initial training should focus on the major modifications to the fundamentals during quick fire.

Dry-Fire Exercises. This dry-fire exercise requires no elaborate preparations or range facilities, yet it provides the soldier with an opportunity to learn and practice quick-fire techniques. Repeated dry-fire exercises ensure soldiers can apply the modifications to the fundamentals. Multiple dry-fire exercises are needed, emphasizing a consistent firing position and weapon alignment with the target, followed by rapid trigger squeeze. No more than one second should elapse between the appearance of the target and a bullet striking it. One example of a dry-fire exercise is:

The trainer/coach places an E-type silhouette target 15 meters in front of the soldier. The soldier stands facing the general direction of the target (vary direction to simulate targets appearing at different locations), holding his rifle at or above waist level. His firing hand should be on the pistol grip; the nonfiring hand cradling the rifle under the handguards.

The trainer/coach should stand slightly behind the soldier, out of his field of view. The trainer/coach claps his hands, signaling target appearance. Immediately after clapping his hands, the trainer/coach counts out loud "one thousand one."

The soldier must either point or aim, squeeze the trigger, and hear the hammer fall before the trainer/coach finishes speaking (about one second or less).

NOTE: When using the aiming technique, the soldier holds his aim and confirms alignment of the rifle with the target. He keeps the rifle pointed toward the target after the hammer falls and looks through the sights to check his actual point of aim for that shot.

Live-Fire Exercises. There are two types of live-fire exercises.

Individual. Emphasis is on engaging each target in one second or less. The previously described timing technique may be used, or pop-up targets set to lock in the full upright position may be used. Pop-up targets require about one second to move from the down to the full up position. Targets set to lock in the upright position must be engaged as they are being raised to "kill" them. This gives the soldier a one-second time limit. At 15 meters (the maximum recommended range), an E-type silhouette engaged using pointed quick fire may be hit anywhere. Using aimed quick fire at the same target, hits should fall within a 10-inch circle located center of target.

NOTE: Repeated live-fire exercises are necessary to train the soldier. If 5.56-mm service ammunition is in short supply, the 5.56-mm practice ammunition and M2 bolt or the .22-caliber rim fire adapter device may be used.

Unit. Unit MOUT LFXs should include the use of quick fire. Targets should be presented at 25 meters or less and soldiers must engage them within one second.

Section V. MOPP FIRING

All soldiers must effectively fire their weapons to accomplish combat missions in an NBC environment. With proper training and practice, soldiers can gain confidence in their ability to effectively hit targets in full MOPP equipment. MOPP firing proficiency must be a part of every unit's training program.

EFFECTS OF MOPP EQUIPMENT ON FIRING

Firing weapons is only part of overall NBC training. Soldiers must first be familiar with NBC equipment, its use, and proper wear before they progress to learning the techniques of MOPP firing. Trainers must consider the impact of MOPP equipment (hood/ mask, gloves, overgarments) on the soldier's ability to properly apply the fundamentals of marksmanship and combat firing skills.

Immediate Action. Under normal conditions a soldier should be able to clear a stoppage in three to five seconds. Under full MOPP, however, this may take as long as ten seconds to successfully complete. Dry-fire practice under these conditions is necessary to reduce time and streamline actions. Hood/mask and gloves must be worn. Care must be taken not to snag or damage the gloves or dislodge the hood/mask during movements. Applying immediate action to a variety of stoppages during dry fire must be practiced using dummy or blank ammunition until such actions can be performed by instinct.

Target Detection. Techniques and principles outlined in Chapter 3 remain valid for target detection while in MOPP, but considerations must be made for limiting factors imposed by MOPP equipment.

Vision is limited to what can be seen through the mask lenses/faceplate. Peripheral vision is severely restricted. The lenses/faceplate may be scratched or partly fogged, thus further restricting vision. Soldiers requiring corrective lenses must be issued insert lenses before training.

Scanning movement may be restricted by the hood/mask. Any of these factors could adversely affect the soldier's ability to quickly and accurately detect targets. Additional skill practice should be conducted.

Marksmanship Fundamentals. Although the four marksmanship fundamentals remain valid during MOPP firing, some modifications may be needed to accommodate the equipment.

Steady position. Due to the added bulk of the overgarments, firing positions may need adjustment for stability and comfort. Dry and live firing while standing, crouching, or squatting may be necessary to reduce body contact with contaminated ground or foliage. A consistent spot/stock weld is difficult to maintain due to the shape of the protective masks. This requires the firer to hold his head in an awkward position to place the eye behind the sight.

Aiming. The wearing of a protective mask may force firers to rotate (cant) the rifle a certain amount to see through the rear aperture. The weapon should be rotated the least amount to properly see through and line up the sights, as previously discussed in Chapter 3. The center tip of the front sight post should be placed on the ideal aiming point. This ideal aiming procedure (Figure 4-7, page 4-16) should be the initial procedure taught and practiced. If this cannot be achieved, a canted sight picture may be practiced.

Breath control. Breathing is restricted and more difficult while wearing the protective mask. Physical exertion can produce labored breathing and make settling down into a normal breath control routine much more difficult. More physical effort is needed to move around when encumbered by MOPP equipment, which can increase the breath rate. All of these factors make holding and controlling the breath to produce a well-aimed shot more energy- and time-consuming. Emphasis must be placed on rapid target engagement during the limited amount of time a firer can control his breath.

Trigger squeeze. Grasping the pistol grip and squeezing the trigger with the index finger are altered when the firer is wearing MOPP gloves. The action of the trigger finger is restricted, and the fit of the glove may require the release of the swing-down trigger guard. Because the trigger feels different, control differs from that used in bare-handed firing. This difference cannot be accurately predicted. Dry-fire training using dime (washer) exercises is necessary to ensure the firer knows the changes he will encounter during live fire.

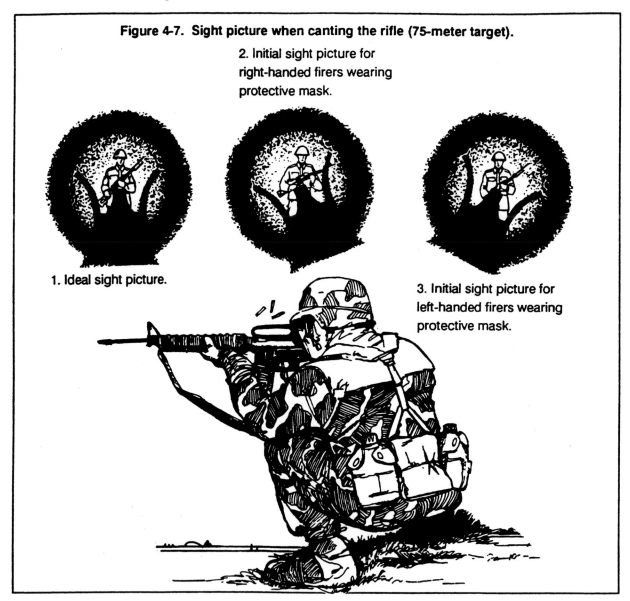

Figure 4-7. Sight picture when canting the rifle (75-meter target).

2. Initial sight picture for right-handed firers wearing protective mask.

1. Ideal sight picture.

3. Initial sight picture for left-handed firers wearing protective mask.

EFFECTS OF AIMING MODIFICATIONS

The normal amount of cant needed by most firers to properly see through the sights has a limited influence on rounds fired at ranges of 75 meters or less. At longer ranges, however, the change in bullet strike becomes more pronounced.

Rifle ballistics (Appendix F) causes the strike of the bullet to impact low in the direction of the cant (when a cant is used) at longer ranges. Due to this shift in bullet strike and the many individual differences in sight alignment when wearing a protective mask, it is important to conduct downrange feedback training (Appendix G) at ranges beyond 75 meters. This allows soldiers to determine what aiming adjustments are needed to achieve center target hits. Figure 4-8 shows what might be expected for a right-handed firer engaging a target at 175 meters with no cant, a certain amount of cant, and the adjustment in point of aim needed to move the bullet strike to the center of the target. Figure 4-9 shows what might be expected for a right-handed firer engaging a 300-meter target. (The adjustments in point of aim for left-handed firers are the opposite of those shown in Figures 4-8 and 4-9.)

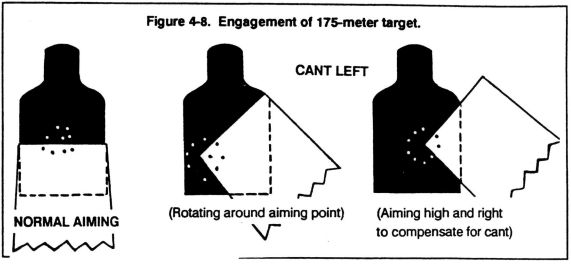

Figure 4-8. Engagement of 175-meter target.

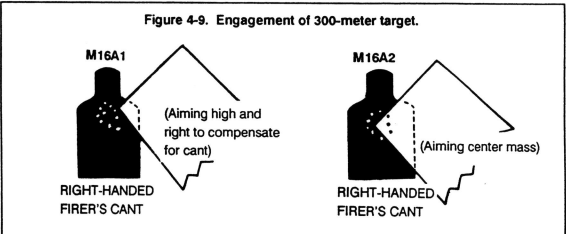

Figure 4-9. Engagement of 300-meter target.

Although bullet strike is displaced when using a cant, individual differences are such that center-of-mass aiming should be used until the individual knows what aiming adjustment is needed. When distant targets are missed, a right-handed firer should usually adjust his point of aim to the right and high; a left-handed firer should adjust to the left and high. Then, the aiming rules are clear. All targets should initially be engaged by aiming center mass, regardless of cant. When targets are missed while using a cant, firers should adjust the point of aim higher and opposite the direction of the cant. Actual displacement of the aiming point must be determined by using downrange feedback targets at ranges beyond 75 meters.

OPERATION AND FUNCTION MODIFICATIONS

Handling the rifle, performing operation and function checks, loading and unloading, and cleaning are affected by MOPP equipment. Movements are slowed, tasks take longer to complete and often require more effort, vision is impaired, and care is needed to avoid damaging MOPP equipment and possible exposure to lethal agents. Because of the great differences between no MOPP and MOPP4, soldiers must be trained in all aspects of operation and maintenance of the weapon while practicing at the highest MOPP level. Only through repeated training and practice can the soldier be expected to perform all tasks efficiently.

MOPP FIRE EXERCISES

The many difficulties the soldier encounters while firing with MOPP gear must be experienced and overcome during training.

Dry-Fire MOPP Exercises. Repeated dry-fire exercises covering all aspects of MOPP firing are the most effective means available to ensure all soldiers can function during a live-fire MOPP situation. Multiple dry-fire exercises must be conducted before the first live round is fired. Otherwise, valuable ammunition and training time are wasted in trying to teach soldiers the basics. The soldier is trained in the fundamentals; repeated dry-fire or Weaponeer exercises are conducted; grouping, zeroing, qualifying, and evaluating are performed using standard non-MOPP firing; the differences and modifications are trained for MOPP firing; and repeated MOPP dry-fire exercises are conducted. The soldier is now ready to move on to MOPP live fire.

Live-Fire MOPP Exercises. These exercises further develop the learned firing skills and allow the soldier to experience the effects of wearing MOPP equipment on downrange performance.

Individual. Application of immediate action, rapid magazine changes, grouping, and adjusted point of aim at 25 meters should all be tested and evaluated for further training. After soldiers exhibit proficiency at these tasks, further training and evaluation at extended ranges are indicated.

Unit. Parts of unit LFXs should be conducted in the highest MOPP level with a planned system of target hit evaluation. As in all aspects of marksmanship training, the emphasis is on soldier knowledge and skills displayed.

Basic 25-meter proficiency course. Initial live-fire exercises are conducted at 25 meters. This training provides all soldiers the basic techniques and introduces firing the rifle in MOPP equipment. This basic proficiency exercise must be fired while wearing gloves and protective mask with hood. The basic 25-meter proficiency exercise is fired to standard and is an annual/semiannual GO/NO-GO requirement for most soldiers. It is entered on the record fire scorecard when completed.

The course of fire can be conducted on any range equipped with mechanical target lifters. Soldiers are given initial instruction and a demonstration of the techniques of firing in MOPP equipment.

Each soldier is issued 20 rounds of 5.56-mm ball ammunition to engage 20 three-to-five-second exposures of F-type silhouette targets at 25 meters. Initial firing is performed with 10 rounds from the individual fighting position (supported), and 10 rounds from a prone unsupported position. Each soldier must obtain a minimum of 11 target hits out of 20 exposures to meet the basic requirement. This initial basic 25-meter exercise prepares soldiers for future individual and unit training in full MOPP gear.

Downrange feedback. Once the soldier has mastered basic marksmanship proficiency, he should be introduced to firing at range. This phase of firing should provide the maximum hit-and-miss performance feedback; it can be conducted on a KD or modified field fire range at 75, 175, and 300 meters.

Practice firing under full MOPP can also be conducted on the standard RETS ranges—for example, the standard record fire tables may be fired in MOPP. MOPP fire must also be part of unit tactical exercises, which are fired on MPRC as part of STXs.

NOTE: The .22-caliber rimfire adapter or plastic practice ammunition may be used during live-fire practice at scaled 25-meter targets when 5.56-mm ammunition is not available.

When the rimfire adapter, plastic ammunition, or live-fire range is not available, the Weaponeer device may be used. Scaled silhouette targets may also be used at this distance to introduce the many target sizes common at longer ranges. The slow-fire target and course outlined in Appendix E are appropriate.

Having mastered the 25-meter firing phase, the soldier is then introduced to firing at range, using the standard 75-, 175-, and 300-meter downrange feedback targets (Chapter 3). Adjusted point of aim, for individual differences of cant, is first used during this training. Live-fire training is conducted on a KD or modified field fire range, giving the soldier feedback on targets engaged at many ranges.

Section VI. MOVING TARGET ENGAGEMENT

The enemy normally moves by rushes from one covered or concealed position to another. While making the rush, the enemy soldier presents a rapidly moving target However, for a brief time as he begins, movement is slow since many steps are needed to gain speed. Many steps are needed to slow down at the new position. A moving target is open to aimed fire both times.

MOVING TARGET TECHNIQUES

There are two primary techniques of engaging moving targets.

Tracking. Tracking is a more accurate technique of engaging targets by experienced firers. It involves the establishment and maintaining of the aiming point in relationship to the target and maintaining that sight picture (moving with the target) while squeezing the trigger. As the target moves, this technique puts the firer in position for a second shot if the first one misses.

Trapping. Trapping is the setting up of an aiming point forward of the target and along the target path. The trigger is squeezed as the target comes into the sights. This is a technique that works on targets with slow lateral movement. It does not require tracking skills. It does require that the firer know precisely when the rifle is going to fire. Some soldiers can squeeze the trigger without reacting to the rifle firing, and they may fire better using this technique.

Another technique is to use a modified 25-meter scaled timed-fire silhouette (see Figure 4-10). Trainers evaluate performance based on where shot groups are placed when the lead rule is applied. This target can be used for both the M16A1 and M16A2 rifles.

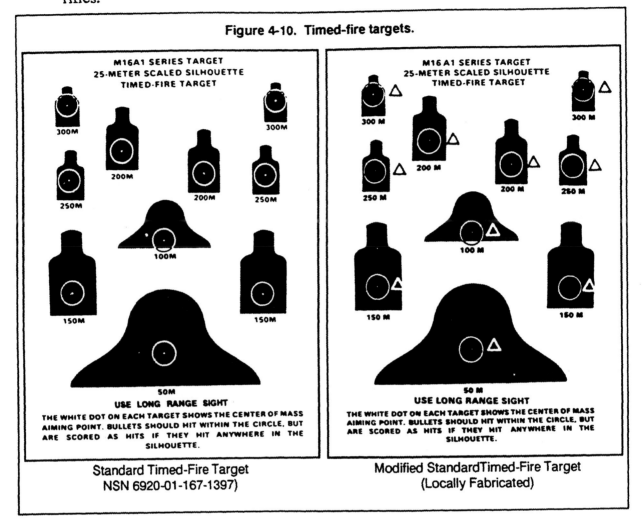

Figure 4-10. Timed-fire targets.

MOVING TARGET FUNDAMENTALS

The fundamentals needed to hit moving targets are similar to those needed to hit stationary targets. The main skill is to engage moving targets with the least changes to procedures. Another consideration is that soldiers in a combat defensive position do not know if their next target will be stationary or moving—they must fire immediately at whatever targets occur.

The fundamentals for engaging stationary targets are steady position, aiming, breath control, and trigger squeeze. They are also used to engage moving targets. Considering the environment and the variables of the rifle and ammunition, the well-trained soldier should be able to hit 300-meter stationary silhouette targets with a .5 PH. When the target has lateral movement, hits at 150 meters may be seven out of ten times, which is a good performance. Therefore, twice as much variability, twice as much dispersion, and a few more erratic shots are expected when soldiers are trained to hit moving targets.

The procedures used to engage moving targets vary as the angle and speed of the target vary. For example, when a moving target is moving directly at the firer, the same procedures are used as would be used if the target were stationary. However, if it is a close, fast-moving target at a 90-degree angle, the rifle and entire upper body of the firer must be free from support so that the target can be tracked. To hit moving targets, the firer must move the rifle smoothly and steadily as the target moves. The front sight post is placed with the trailing edge at target center, breath is held, and the trigger is squeezed. Several factors complicate this process.

Steady position. When firing from a firing position, the firer is in the standard supported position and is flexible enough to track any target in his sector. When a moving target is moving directly at the firer, directly away, or at a slight angle, the target is engaged without changing the firing position. When targets have much lateral movement, only minor changes are needed to allow for effective target engagement. Most moving targets are missed in the horizontal plane (firing in front of or behind the target) and not in the vertical plane (firing too low or too high). Therefore, a smooth track is needed on the target, even if the support arm must be lifted. Other adjustments include the following:

- *Nonfiring hand.* The grip of the nonfiring hand may need to be increased and more pressure applied to the rear. This helps to maintain positive control of the rifle and steady it for rapid trigger action.
- *Nonfiring elbow.* The elbow is lifted from the support position only to maintain a smooth track.
- *Grip of the right hand.* Rearward pressure may be applied to the pistol grip to steady the rifle during trigger squeeze.
- *Firing elbow.* The firing elbow is lifted from support only to help maintain a smooth track.

NOTE: The rifle pocket on the shoulder and the stock weld are the same for stationary targets.

Aiming. The trailing edge of the front sight post is at target center.
Breath control. Breathing is locked at the moment of trigger squeeze.
Trigger squeeze. Rearward pressure on the handguard and pistol grip is applied to hold the rifle steady while pressure is applied to the trigger. The trigger is squeezed fast (almost a controlled jerk). Heavy pressure is applied on the trigger (at least half the pressure it takes to make the rifle fire) before squeezing the trigger.

SINGLE-LEAD RULE FOR MOVING TARGETS

A target moving directly toward the firer can be engaged the same way as a stationary target. However, to hit a target moving laterally, the firer places the trailing edge of the front sight sight post at target center. The sight-target relationship is shown in Figure 4-11(page 4-22). The single-lead rule automatically increases the lead as the range to the target increases.

Figure 4-12 (page 4-22) shows how this works, with the front sight post covering about 1.6 inches at 15 meters and about 16 inches at 150 meters. Since the center of the front sight post is the actual aiming point, this technique of placing the trailing edge of the front sight post at target center provides for an .8-inch lead on a 15-meter target, and an 8-inch lead on a target at 150 meters.

This rules provides for a dead-center hit on a 15-meter target that is moving at 7 mph at a 25-degree angle because the target moves .8 inch between the time the rifle is fired and the bullet arrives at the target. A 150-meter target moving at 7 mph at a 25-degree angle moves 8 inches between the time the weapon is fired and the bullet arrives. This rule provides for hits on the majority of high-priority combat targets.

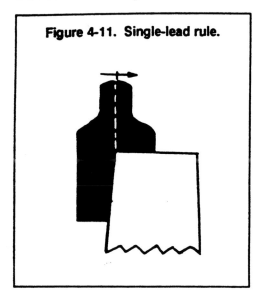

Figure 4-11. Single-lead rule.

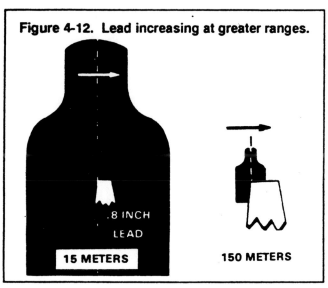

Figure 4-12. Lead increasing at greater ranges.

LEAD REQUIREMENTS

To effectively engage moving targets on the battlefield, soldiers must understand lead requirements. Figure 4-13 shows the amount of lead required to hit a 300-meter target when it is moving 8 mph at an angle of 90 degrees. Aiming directly at the target would result in missing it. When an enemy soldier is running 8 mph, 90 degrees to the firer, and at a range of 300 meters, he covers 4 1/2 feet while the bullet is traveling toward him. To get a hit, the firer must aim and fire at position D when the enemy is at position A. This indicates the need for target lead and for marksmanship trainers to know bullet speed and how it relates to the range, angle, and speed of the target. Soldiers must understand that targets moving fast and laterally are led by some distance if they are to be hit.

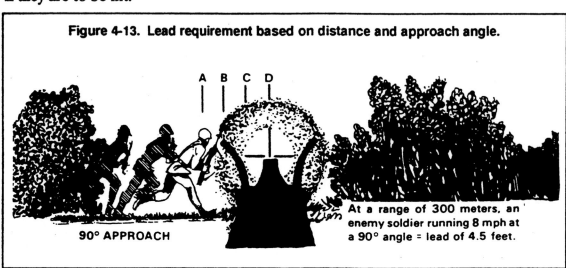

Figure 4-13. Lead requirement based on distance and approach angle.

90° APPROACH

At a range of 300 meters, an enemy soldier running 8 mph at a 90° angle = lead of 4.5 feet.

Target Speed. Figure 4-14 reflects the differences in lateral speed for various angles of target movement for a target that is traveling at 8 mph at a distance of 150 meters from the firer. The angle of target movement is the angle between the target-firer line and the target's direction of movement. An 8-mph target moves 24 inches during the bullet's flight time. If the target is moving on a 15-degree angle, it moves 6 inches (the equivalent of 2 mph). For the firer to apply precise lead rules, he must accurately estimate speed, angle, and range to the target during the enemy soldier's brief exposure. The single-lead rule (place the trailing edge of the front sight post at target center) places effective fire on most high-priority combat targets. At 100 meters, the rule begins to break down for targets moving at slight and large angles.

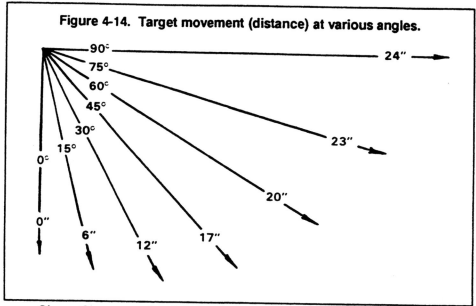

Figure 4-14. Target movement (distance) at various angles.

Since the target lead is half the perceived width of the front sight post, at 100 meters the standard sight provides for 5.4 inches of lead for the M16A1 and M16A2 front sights (Figure 4-15, page 4-24).

Target Distance. The front sight post covers only a small part of close-in targets, providing for target hits on close targets moving at any angle and any speed. However, if the lead rule is applied on more distant targets moving at a slight angle — for example, 5 degrees at 100 meters — the bullet strikes forward of target center, about 4 inches with standard sights and about 7 inches with LLLSS sights. Therefore, soldiers are taught to fire at targets as though they are stationary until lateral movement is observed (15 degrees).

The rule provides for many speed-angle combinations that place the bullet within 2 inches of target center (Figure 4-16, page 4-25). Since the soldier is expected to fire a 12-inch group on moving targets at 100 meters, the rule provides for hits on the majority of targets. Even the worst case (a 90-degree target moving at 8 mph) would result in the shot-group center being located 9.8 inches behind target center. If bullets were evenly distributed within a 12-inch group, this would result in hitting the target 40 percent of the time.

Soldiers should be taught to increase their lead when targets are missed. This increases their probability of hitting all targets. The amount of additional lead required

Figure 4-15. Angle of target movement.

ANGLE OF TARGET MOVEMENT	RANGE: 100 METERS		
	(STANDARD SIGHT) TARGET SPEED		
	4 MPH	6 MPH	8 MPH
5°	+4.9"	+4.5"	+4.3"
10°	+4.1"	+3.5"	+2.7"
15°	+3.5"	+2.5"	+1.5"
20°	+2.8"	+1.5"	+.2"
25°	+2.2"	+.7"	-1.0"
30°	+1.7"	-.2"	-2.0"
35°	+1.1"	-1.1"	-3.2"
40°	+.6"	-1.9"	-4.3"
45°		-2.7"	-5.4"
50°	-.4"	-3.3"	-6.2"
55°	-.8"	-4.0"	-7.0"
60°	-1.2"	-4.5"	-7.7"
65°	-1.5"	-4.9"	-8.4"
70°	-1.7"	-5.3"	-8.8"
75°	-1.9"	-5.6"	-9.2"
80°	-2.0"	-5.9"	-9.6"
85°	-2.1"	-5.9"	-9.7"
90°	-2.1"	-6.0"	-9.8"

NOTE: Plus (+) indicates bullet strike in the direction of movement; minus (-) indicates bullet strike behind the target center.

should be developed through experience with only general guidance provided. For example, if there is much lateral movement of the target and the soldier feels by applying the lead rule and firing fundamentals he has missed the target, then he should increase his lead.

The training program must be simple and provide soldiers with only relevant information to improve their performance in combat. First, all soldiers should understand and apply the single-lead rule in the absence of more information. Second, soldiers should understand that moving targets coming toward them or on a slight angle (0 to 15 degrees) should be engaged as stationary targets. Third, information should be presented and practice allowed on applying additional lead to targets for soldiers who demonstrate an aptitude for this skill.

Target Angle. The rule does not apply to targets moving at small and large angles (Figure 4-16). For example, a walking enemy soldier at 250 meters is hit dead center when he is moving at 40 degrees. Hits can be obtained if he is moving on any angle between 15 and 75 degrees. When he is running (a center hit is obtained when the target is on an angle of 18 degrees), misses occur when he exceeds an angle of 30 to 35 degrees. The information provided in Figures 4-13, page 4-23, and 4-14, page 4-24, is designed to enhance instructor understanding so proper concepts are presented during instruction. For example, a target at 100 meters moving at 6 mph receives a center hit when moving at 29 degrees. When moving at an angle less than 29 degrees, the bullet strikes somewhat in front of target center. When moving at an angle of more than 29 degrees, the bullet strikes somewhat behind target center.

Figure 4-16. Target angle when dead center: hits accure using single lead rule.

(STANDARD SIGHT)

RANGE	4 MPH	6 MPH	8 MPH
25M	48°	30ᶜ	22ᶜ
50M	47°	30ᶜ	22ᶜ
100M	45ᶜ	29ᶜ	21°
150M	44ᶜ	28ᶜ	20ᶜ
200M	41°	27°	19ᶜ
250M	40°	26°	18ᶜ
300M	33°	21°	16°
350M	38°	24°	18°
400M	35°	22ᶜ	17ᶜ
450M	33°	21ᶜ	16ᶜ

MULTIPURPOSE RANGE COMPLEX TRAIN-UP

MPRCs require soldiers to hit moving targets. Ranges are used for collective training. Commanders should try to use the MPRCs for individual training and to teach the individual to engage moving targets. If no MPRCs are available for individual training, any range can be used that will support any type of moving target. Building a moving target range is limited only by the imagination of the trainer, but always within safety constraints. The following are examples that can be incorporated on many ranges.

Popsicle Sticks. This requires placing an E-type silhouette on a long stick and having an individual walk back and forth behind a high berm (high enough to protect the individual from fire) the length of the berm. Feedback should be made available for the firer such as for lowering the target when a hit is scored or reversing direction upon a hit.

Sled Targets. This requires constructing a simple sled that has one or more targets attached. The sled is pulled by a rope or cable across and off the range safely by a vehicle.

CHAPTER 5

Night Firing

All units must be able to fight during limited visibility. All soldiers should know the procedures for weapons employment during such time. Soldiers must experience the various conditions of night combat—from total darkness, to the many types of artificial illumination, to the use of surveillance aids. All units must include basic, unassisted night fire training annually in their unit marksmanship programs. Combat units should conduct tactical night fire training at least quarterly. This tactical training should include MILES during force-on-force training as well as live fire. Night-fire training must include the use of applicable night vision devices when this equipment is part of a TOE. The many effects darkness has on night firing are discussed herein.

NOTE: Although this chapter addresses night firing, the appropriate modifications to the fundamentals of firing may be applied whenever visibility is limited.

CONSIDERATIONS

Trainers must consider the impact of limited visibility on the soldier's ability to properly apply the fundamentals of marksmanship and combat firing skills. These fundamentals/ skills include:

Operation and Maintenance of the Weapon. Handling the weapon, performing operation and function checks, loading and unloading, and maintenance are affected by nighttime conditions. Movements are slowed, tasks take longer to complete, vision is impaired, and equipment is more easily misplaced or lost. Because combat conditions and enforcement of noise and light discipline restrict the use of illumination, soldiers must be trained to operate (load, unload, and clear), service, and clean their weapons using the lowest lighting conditions. Although initial practice of these tasks should occur during daylight (using simulated darkness) to facilitate control and error correction, repeated practice during actual nighttime conditions should be integrated with other training. Only through repeated practice and training can the soldier be expected to perform all tasks efficiently.

Immediate Action. Under normal conditions, a soldier should clear a stoppage in three to five seconds. After dark, this task usually takes longer. Identifying the problem may be frustrating and difficult for the soldier. A tactile (hands only) technique of identifying a stoppage must be taught and practiced. Clearing the stoppage using few or no visual indicators must also be included. The firer must apply immediate action with his eyes closed. Dry-fire practice using dummy or blank rounds under these conditions is necessary to reduce time and build confidence. Training should be practiced first during daylight for better control and error correction by the trainer. Practice during darkness can be simulated by closing the eyes or using a blindfold. Once the soldier is confident in applying immediate action in daylight or darkness, he can perform such actions rapidly on the firing line.

Target Detection. Many of the skills discussed in Appendix B apply to target detection after dark. Light from a cigarette or flashlight, discharge of a rifle (muzzle flash), or reflected moonlight/starlight are the main means of target location. Sounds may also be indicators of target areas. Because the other techniques of detection (movement, contrast) are less apparent at night, light and sound detection must be taught, trained, and reviewed repeatedly in practice exercises. Exercises should also emphasize shortened scanning ranges, night vision adaptation, and use of off-center vision. Target detection exercises should be integrated into all collective training tasks.

NOTE: Binoculars are often overlooked as night vision aids. Because they amplify the available light, binoculars or spotting/rifle scopes can provide the firer with another means to locate targets during limited visibility. Also, the use of MILES equipment is effective for use in engaging detected targets.

Marksmanship Fundamentals. The four marksmanship fundamentals apply to night firing. Some modifications are needed depending on the conditions. The firer must still place effective fire on the targets or target areas that have been detected.

Steady position. When the firer is firing unassisted, changes in his head position/stock weld will be necessary, especial when using weapon-target alignment techniques. When using rifle-mounted night vision devices, head position/stock weld must be changed to bring the firing eye in line with the device. Also, such mounted devices alter the rifle's weight and center of gravity, forcing a shift in placement of the support (nonfiring arm or sandbags). Repeated dry-fire practice, followed by live-fire training, is necessary to learn and refine these modifications and still achieve the most steady position.

Aiming. Modifications to the aiming process vary from very little (when using LLLSSs) to extensive (when using modified quick-fire techniques). When firing unassisted, the firer's off-center vision is used instead of pinpoint focus. When using a mounted night vision device, the firer's conventional iron sights are not used. The soldier uses the necessary aiming process to properly use the device.

Breathing. Weapon movement caused by breathing becomes more apparent when using night vision devices that magnify the field of view. This fundamental is not greatly affected by night fire conditions.

Trigger squeeze. This important fundamental does not change during night fire. The objective is to not disrupt alignment of the weapon with the target.

PRINCIPLES OF NIGHT VISION
For a soldier to effectively engage targets at night, he must apply the three principles of night vision:

Dark Adaptation. Moving from lighted to darkened areas (as in leaving a tent) can be temporarily blinding. After several minutes have passed, the soldier can slowly see his surroundings. If he remains in this completely darkened environment, he adapts to the dark in about 30 minutes. This does not mean he can see in the dark at the end of this time. After about 30 minutes, his visibility reaches its maximum level. If light is encountered, the eyes must adapt again. The fire on the end of a cigarette or a red-lensed flashlight can degrade night vision; larger light sources cause more severe losses.

Off-Center Vision. During the day, the soldier focuses his vision on the object he wants to see. Shifting this pinpoint focus slightly to one side causes the object to become blurry or lose detail. At night, the opposite is true. Focusing directly on an object after dark results in that object being visible for only a few seconds. After that, the object becomes almost invisible. To view an object at night, the soldier must shift his gaze slightly to one side. This allows the light-sensitive parts of the eye (parts not used during daylight) to be used. These can detect faint light sources or reflections and relay their image to the brain. (Figures 5-1 and 5-2.)

NOTE: Vision is shifted slightly to one side, but attention is still on the object. Because of the blind spot at the center of vision, directing attention to an off-centered objective is possible (with practice).

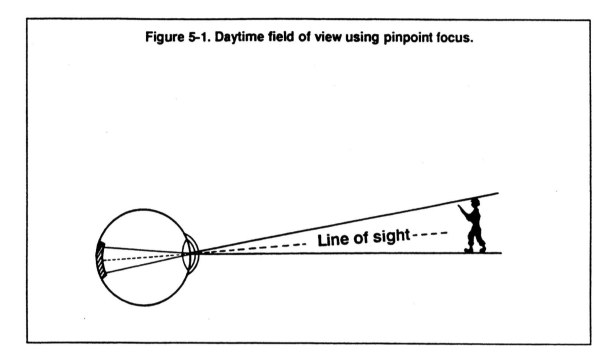

Figure 5-1. Daytime field of view using pinpoint focus.

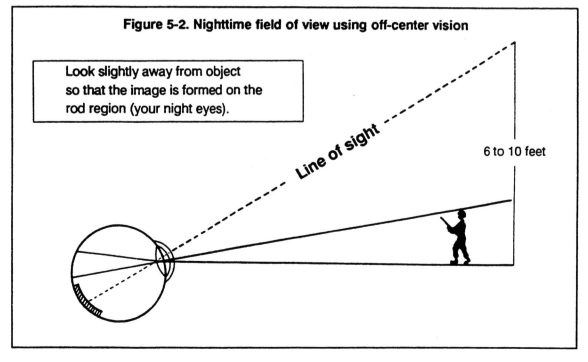

Figure 5-2. Nighttime field of view using off-center vision

Look slightly away from object so that the image is formed on the rod region (your night eyes).

6 to 10 feet

Scanning. Scanning is the short, abrupt, irregular movement of the soldier's eyes around an object or area every 4 to 10 seconds. Off-center vision is used. Scanning ranges vary according to visibility.

NOTE: For detailed information on the three principles, see FM 21-75.

TARGET ENGAGEMENT TECHNIQUES
Night fire usually occurs under three general conditions.

Unassisted Firing Exercise. The firer must detect and engage targets without artificial illumination or night vision devices. Potential target areas are scanned. When a target is detected, the firer should engage it using a modified quick-fire position. His head is positioned high so that he is aligning the weapon on the target and looking just over the iron sights. His cheek should remain in contact with the stock.

The firer should take a few seconds to improve weapon/target alignment by pointing slightly low to compensate for the usual tendency to fire high. Both eyes are open to the maximum advantage of any available light, and the focus is downrange. Off-center vision is used to keep the target in sight. Tracer ammunition may provide feedback on the line of trajectory and facilitate any adjustments in weapon/target alignment.

Repeated dry-fire training, target detection, and proper aiming practice are the most efficient means to ensure the soldier can successfully engage short-range targets (50 meters or closer) unassisted during MILES exercises, and then live-fire training.

Artificial Illumination. Targets as distant as 175 meters can be engaged successfully with some type of artificial illumination. Illumination may be from hand flares, mortar or artillery fire, or bright incandescent lights such as searchlights.

When artificial illumination is used, the eyes lose most of their night adaption, and off-center vision is no longer useful. Aiming is accomplished as it is during the day. Artificial illumination allows the firer to use the iron sights as he does during the day. (M16A2 users should keep the large rear sight aperture flipped up during darkness.)

Engaging targets under artificial illumination allows for better target detection and long-range accuracy than the unassisted technique. When the light is gone, time must be spent in regaining night vision and adaptation. Only when the light level drops enough so that the target cannot be seen through the iron sights should the firer resume short-range scanning, looking just over the sights.

Soldiers have sometimes been taught to close their eyes during artificial illumination to preserve their night vision. This technique is effective but also renders the soldier (or entire unit) blind for the duration of the illumination. Keeping one eye closed to preserve its night vision results in a drastically altered sense of perception when both eyes are opened, following the illumination burnout. Tactical considerations should be the deciding factor as to which technique to use. Repeated dry-fire training and target detection practice are the keys to successful engagement of targets out to 150 meters or more during live fire under artificial illumination.

Night Vision Devices. Rifle-mounted night vision devices are the most effective night fire aids. By using these devices, the firer can observe the area, detect and engage any suitable targets, and direct the fire of soldiers who are firing unassisted.

NVDs can be used to engage targets out to 300 meters. Repeated training, dry-fire practice, and correct zeroing are vital to the proper employment of NVDs during live-fire training.

TRAINING
Dry-fire training and live-fire training are necessary to mastering basic rifle marksmanship. The soldier must adhere to the following procedures and applications to be effective in combat.

Dry-Fire Exercises. Repeated training and dry-fire practice are the most effective means available to ensure all soldiers can function efficiently after dark.

Target detection and dry-fire exercises must be conducted before the first live round is fired. They can take place almost anywhere—elaborate live-fire range facilities are not needed. Modified fundamentals can be taught in a classroom/practical exercise situation. Further training in the proper zeroing and engagement techniques can take place anywhere that targets can be set up and darkness can be expected.

Without extensive dry-fire training, soldiers do not perform to standards during live fire. Valuable range time and ammunition are wasted in a final attempt to teach the basics.

The soldier must demonstrate skill during daylight live fire. Next, he is trained in the differences and modifications needed for successful night firing. Many dry-fire exercises are conducted until skill at night firing is displayed. Only then is the soldier ready to move on to the night live-fire exercises.

Live-Fire Exercises. These exercises continue to develop the firing skills acquired during dry-fire exercises, and they allow the soldier to experience the effects of darkness on downrange performance.

The basic unassisted live-fire exercise allows all soldiers to apply night-fire principles, and to gain confidence in their abilities to effectively engage targets at 25 and 50 meters. Practice and proficiency firing can be conducted on any range equipped with mechanical lifters and muzzle flash simulators. A small square of reflective material and a shielded low wattage flashing light (protected from bullet impact) may be used to facilitate target detection. (Figures 5-3, page 5-6) The light should be placed to highlight the center of the target with a flashing, faint glow (intended to represent a muzzle flash). The light should not be on constantly, when the target is not exposed, or on when the target is exposed but not being used in actual engagement. The light should provide the firer with a momentary indication that a target is presenting itself for engagement. It should not be attached to the target or provide the firer with a distinct aiming point, regardless of how dim it may be. Practice can also be accomplished by the use of MILES equipment and target interface devices.

When an automated record fire range (RETS) is used for this exercise, the two 50-meter mechanisms are used. Before training, one E-type silhouette target is replaced with an F-type silhouette target. The F-type silhouette target is engaged at 25 meters from the prone unsupported position. The soldier is issued one magazine of 15 rounds (5 rounds ball; 10 rounds tracer) and presented 15 ten-second exposures. The firing line is moved, and the soldier engages the E-type silhouette target at 50 meters. He is issued a second 15-round magazine (5 rounds ball; 10 rounds tracer) to engage 15 ten-second exposures.

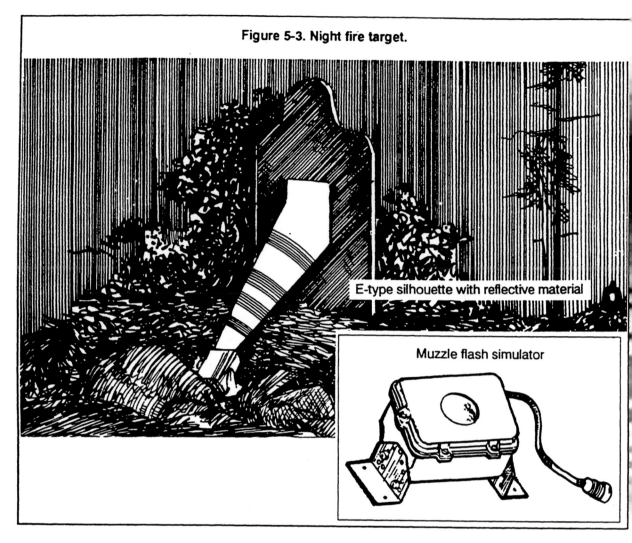

Figure 5-3. Night fire target.

E-type silhouette with reflective material

Muzzle flash simulator

When the automated range is used, the soldier's performance is recorded in the tower. If automatic scoring is not available, F-type and E-type silhouette paper facings are attached to the mechanical target, and bullet holes are counted. Facings may be repaired or replaced for each firer.

To meet the annual/semiannual minimum performance requirements, all soldiers must hit and kill seven separate targets out of 30 exposures. The results are annotated on the soldier's record fire scorecard.

- *Individual.* Application of immediate action, rapid magazine changes, and refinements of the modified quick-fire aiming point should be tested and evaluated for further training.

  - *Unassisted.* After soldiers exhibit proficiency of individual tasks, training and evaluation at ranges beyond those possible using only the rifle are indicated.

  - *Artificial illumination.* After mastering the unassisted night fire task and after repeated dry-fire training under artificial illumination, the soldier is ready to be tested and evaluated using live fire under illumination. Pop-up or stationary targets at ranges out to 175 meters (depending on light conditions, terrain features, and vegetation) may be used. Illumination is provided by flares, mortar/artillery, or floodlights. Once these tasks are mastered, further training and evaluation using NVDs is indicated. Multipurpose range complexes can be used for night firing by using artificial illumination. Automated field fire or record fire ranges can also be used by adding lighting. During this training, soldiers engage targets at 75 to 175 meters. Several target scenarios are possible. A typical training exercise would present 30 random exposures of the 75-meter and 175-meter targets (or optional 100-meter and 200-meter targets). Soldiers should be expected to hit at least 10 targets. Tracer ammunition can be used to enhance training.

– *Night vision devices.* Repeated training and dry-fire practice on the proper use of NVDs are essential to the successful conduct of any live-fire training using these devices. Firers must understand the equipment and skillfully employ it. NVDs can provide engagement capabilities out to 300 meters.

NOTE: Spotlights or floodlights can be modified through use of a rheostat to simulate the flickering, bright/dim nature of artificial illumination. Lights should not be used to continuously spotlight targets. Unanticipated artificial illumination may render NVDs difficult to see through or may shut the device off. Live-fire training should consider any problems incurred by such unexpected illumination.

• *Unit.* Parts of unit STXs, FTXs, and LFXs should be conducted at night. This training should include target detection, unassisted MILES and live fire, artificial illumination, and NVDs. Targets out to 300 meters may be used, depending on the existing conditions. Emphasis is on soldier knowledge and skills displayed.

NOTE: See FM 25-7 for a description of ranges available and recommended for live-fire training.